T0375208

Answers for Christians Today

Biblical Lessons for Living in Christ

NATHAN GARNETT

WESTBOW PRESS®
A DIVISION OF THOMAS NELSON & ZONDERVAN

WestBow Press books may be ordered through booksellers or by contacting:

WestBow Press
A Division of Thomas Nelson & Zondervan
1663 Liberty Drive
Bloomington, IN 47403
www.westbowpress.com
1 (866) 928-1240

ISBN: 978-1-5127-3662-5 (sc)
ISBN: 978-1-5127-3663-2 (hc)
ISBN: 978-1-5127-3661-8 (e)

Library of Congress Control Number: 2016905518

Print information available on the last page.

WestBow Press rev. date: 05/23/2016

To Maddie, Nick, and Josh:

May the Lord grant you wisdom, courage, and the passion to joyfully walk with Him all of your days.

"Walk as children of light (for the fruit of light is found in all that is good and right and true), and try to discern what is pleasing to the Lord."

- Ephesians 5:9-10

My son, if you receive my words
    and treasure up my commandments with you,
making your ear attentive to wisdom
    and inclining your heart to understanding;
yes, if you call out for insight
    and raise your voice for understanding,
if you seek it like silver
    and search for it as for hidden treasures,
then you will understand the fear of the Lord
    and find the knowledge of God.

- Proverbs 2:1-5

Fear God and keep his commandments,
for this is the whole duty of man.

- Ecclesiastes 12:13

Contents

Contents

Acknowledgements

An expression of gratitude is in order for those friends who have helped to improve the quality of this work. Several men provided necessary critique regarding grammar, style, content, and especially doctrinal accuracy. Their support and guidance are greatly appreciated, both for this undertaking and numerous other endeavors.

For encouragement in various ministry-related projects, and for always being available to offer sound advice, I'm thankful to my pastor of over twenty years, David Campbell. To my cousin Darrell Hahn, who has always been more like a brother, I'm grateful for his inspiration and conviction in carrying on the family legacy of serving Christ. Dr. Michael Bryant, a lifelong friend and mentor, has always been a source of encouragement and wise counsel. Chris Wilson has given a substantial amount of effort to this project, and with a genuine pastor's heart he is always ready to give support in whatever way is needed. Long-time friend and fellow author, John Turpin, has offered assistance, accountability, and biblical counsel during so many seasons of my life. And to Jimmy Hazlett, whose willingness to help a new friend is greatly appreciated.

Finally, I am very thankful for my wife, Sherri, who has provided immense support to me. She brings balance to my schedule in order to make sure that our children are not forsaken while I have pursued various endeavors. Her patience, resilience, and exemplary compassion have made her a wonderful partner in life and ministry for over twenty years.

Preface

This book is somewhat unique in that it is not intended to cover a single subject in great depth, but rather it contains a mixture of general overviews on specific topics as well as some fairly deep interactions with outside sources. There are also a variety of formats used throughout, mainly because the chapters began as a compilation of papers written during my years of study in seminary. The goal of that formal education was to provide preparation for practical theological application in the context of a local church, so my professors intentionally assigned research topics that are of significant concern to contemporary Christians. Hence, the book's title suggests that the issues addressed herein are particularly relevant for "Christians today."

Not only does the subject matter vary throughout, but there are numerous types of writings which serve different purposes. Some chapters stem from research papers in which the objective was to simply convey data from various sources in an understandable and useful manner. Other portions contain somewhat technical arguments in which the original Greek text was used to bring out a deeper and more accurate interpretation of a biblical passage. Yet another type of work you will find here is the position paper, which consists of arguments from various points of view and an assessment of whose position I consider to be the most biblical. Lastly, there is included a bonus chapter which does not fully answer a question but still provides "food for thought." Regardless of the type of paper, and whether or not an issue is fully debated or resolved, all of the chapters in this book draw from numerous reputable sources which I highly recommend reading for yourself.

Generally, the chapters are arranged in order of necessity. Topics related to the most basic, and most important, Christian doctrines are included at the beginning. These matters are essential to a person coming to know Jesus Christ as his or her personal Savior. The latter chapters discuss topics which are not as important with regard to salvation, but they do offer value in developing spiritual maturity. So, if you are like me in habitually starting a book yet never quite making it to the end, then at least here you will acquire the most essential information before turning aside to some other activity.

The original intention of the book was to preserve for my own family some instruction that may be of practical use, so that my efforts in seminary could accomplish more than simply a grade for a class. As I began to select which writings to include, however, it became evident that there is a larger audience who may benefit from this work. As is common today, many of us have numerous questions but do not have time to study a multitude of topics at length. Moreover, even the best expositional preachers and teachers in our churches cannot feasibly provide substantial depth with regard to every Christian doctrine. It is my hope that this work will lay some basic foundations for each topic, and that the extensive references cited will help the reader to find more detail if so desired. This book should therefore be a good resource for pastors, church members, and even those who have not yet embraced the Christian faith. May the Lord bless you with wisdom as you seek answers to these five common questions.

Question 1

How Did We Get the New Testament?

Part 1: Composition

Introduction

Foundational to Christian faith are the Scriptures contained within the Bible. If you call yourself a Christian, then you learned of Jesus Christ and placed your trust in him for salvation because the Bible revealed the truth of his identity to you. As a Christian, you find purpose in life and develop moral standards for how you will live that life, because the Bible informs you of what God requires. And when you face a multitude of challenges in life you find the greatest source of hope in God's character, which is revealed in the Bible. Everything you believe about yourself, your Creator, and the world in which you live is based upon your own understanding of God's message which was preserved for you in the pages of the Bible.

In order for us to appreciate and utilize God's Word, however, we need to be confident that it contains exactly what he wants to convey – no more and no less. And of particular importance to Christ-followers are the New Testament books, which were written by authors with firsthand knowledge of Jesus Christ. The first part of this chapter will address the composition of the New Testament, describing how we actually received it. This will be done primarily by explaining the materials and methods that were employed in physically preserving God's written words. Part 1 will then conclude with a brief summary of the historical setting which brought about the need for compiling a limited group of writings that are still present today in our New Testament. This will set the stage for Part 2, which covers in detail the process by which these specific books were identified as Holy Scripture.

Writing Materials and Terminology

Almost all New Testament writings were on papyrus or parchment.[1] The term *papyrus*, of Latin descent from the Greek *papuros*, refers to a reed plant that grew along the Nile River in Egypt.[2] The German and French adapted this word as *papier*, from which the English derived *paper*. Another term used for papyrus was *bublos*, which was later spelled *biblos*. This alternate spelling is attributed to the Syrian port, Byblos, from which much of the papyrus production was exported.[3] The Greek word *biblion*, meaning "rolled up papyrus," was later used to describe books. Eventually, and through several more language adaptations, the English settled on the term *Bible* to describe the compilation of Holy Scriptures.

From about BC 3000 to BC 200 the primary media available for writing upon was papyrus. But when an embargo halted shipments, the need arose for an alternative. *Parchment* was then developed and named after the city of its origin; Pergamum in Asia Minor. Less expensive animal skins for use as parchment included older cattle, sheep, goats, and

---

[1] Bruce M. Metzger. *The Text of the New Testament: Its Transmission, Corruption, and Restoration.* 2nd ed. (New York: Oxford University Press, 1981), 3.

[2] F.F. Bruce. *The Books and the Parchments.* Revised Edition. (London: HarperCollins, 1991), 3.

[3] David Ewert. From Ancient Tablets to Modern Translations: A General Introduction to the Bible. (Grand Rapids: Zondervan, 1983), 20.

antelope.[4] The finest, more expensive parchments were made from calfskin and were named *vellum.*[5]

A *scroll* was made by gluing multiple sheets of papyrus or parchment together and then rolling them around a stick. The Latin word for "something rolled up" is *volumen*, from which we derived *volume*. For ease of use these scrolls, or volumes, seldom exceeded thirty-five feet in length. Hence, large literary works would be divided among multiple scrolls. This is the reason one of the New Testament writings was divided into the books of Luke and Acts, as they were each about thirty-two feet in length.[6]

By the early second century, sheets of papyrus or parchment were folded and sewn together at the seam with other sheets, creating the *codex*. Pages of a codex allowed for writing on both sides, so that a single codex could contain more than one volume. The two oldest codices are the Vaticanus and Sinaiticus, dating to the fourth century. These were two of the fifty manuscripts copied by Eusebius in AD 331 for the first Christian emperor, Constantine, to supply his new churches.[7]

Original documents penned by their authors are called *autographs*. Because these were written on papyrus or parchment, which would require exceptional conditions to survive, none exist today.[8] Before their disappearance, however, scribes copied the autographs and the best surviving copies have been used for today's modern Bible translations. But before printing was made possible with the invention of the printing press in AD 1440, all copies were handwritten and thereby earned the name *manuscript.*[9]

To facilitate greater speed, *cursive* (running hand) was used for common, non-literary manuscripts. Formal literary works, however, were written in *uncial* (book hand). This style of writing, used primarily from the third to sixth century, required more deliberate and careful penmanship, with each letter separated from others. Between the sixth and

---

[4] Metzger, *Text of New Testament*, 4.

[5] Bruce, *Books and Parchments*, 4.

[6] Metzger, *Text of New Testament*, 5.

[7] Ibid., 7.

[8] Bruce, *Books and Parchments,* 166.

[9] R.F. Youngblood, F.F. Bruce and R.K. Harrison, ed. *Nelson's New Illustrated Bible Dictionary*. (Nashville: Thomas Nelson, 1995), 189.

ninth centuries, a decline in writing quality spawned the use of smaller letters, called *minuscule*, which then became standard for use in book production. These were a smaller, modified form of the cursive, requiring less space and therefore fewer sheets of the codex. Smaller codices were easier to carry and less expensive to make. Pertaining to New Testament writings, earlier manuscripts contain uncial letters, whereas later writings have the minuscule style. With either method, punctuation was not used consistently until the eighth century. There were also no spaces between words, which was described as *scriptio continua*.[10]

[10] Metzger, *Text of New Testament*, 9-10,13.

The Progression From Greek to English

Matt. 1:2 in the ***uncial*** Codex Basilensis, identified by E[e], was written in the 8th century. It is located at the University of Basel in Basel, Switzerland.

Matt. 1:2 in the ***miniscule*** manuscript identified as 676 or α573, depending on the cataloging system. It was written in the 13th century, and is held at the Bibelmuseum in Munster, Germany.

Compiling text from various manuscripts of Matt. 1:2, and using a contemporary font which resembles miniscule letters:

Ἀβραὰμ ἐγέννησεν τὸν Ἰσαάκ, Ἰσαὰκ δὲ ἐγέννησεν τὸν Ἰακώβ,
Ἰακὼβ δὲ ἐγέννησεν τὸν Ἰούδαν καὶ τοὺς ἀδελφοὺς αὐτοῦ
(Greek New Testament published by the Society of Biblical Literature)

The result of translating this example into an English version of the New Testament:

Abraham was the father of Isaac, Isaac the father of Jacob,
and Jacob the father of Judah and his brothers. (NASB)

Because of the expense of writing media it was common for a piece of parchment to be reused by scraping off the original text. The most significant of these *palimpsests*, which means "re-scraped," was a manuscript named Codex Ephraemi Rescriptus. It was originally written in the fifth century, and reused in the twelfth century. We know this because with special chemicals and lights much of the original writing can be read. Although in AD 692 the Quinisext Council of Trullo banned this practice, fifty-two of our existing 250 uncial New Testament manuscripts are palimpsests.[11]

State sanctioning of Christianity by Emperor Constantine in the fourth century gave rise to commercial book manufacturing. In a monastery room called the *scriptorium*, copying of the New Testament was expedited through the use of several scribes, both Christian and non-Christian, who would write as a *lector* read aloud from the *exemplar*.

Several factors contributed to errors in manuscripts as they were copied. Astigmatism of the eyes caused difficulty distinguishing Greek letters. Also, the use of similar words in close proximity to one another could cause the text between them to be left out. Words read by the lector may have different meanings, and thus a scribe could write the wrong one. Poor memory between reading and writing, or between hearing and writing, could also be problematic. Letters or words could be transposed unintentionally, and notes written in margins were sometimes added to the text.[12] Metzger gives us an example of a scribal error as follows.

> "What is perhaps the most atrocious of all scribal blunders is contained in the 14th century codex 109. This manuscript of the Four Gospels, now in the British Museum, was transcribed from a copy which must have had Luke's genealogy of Jesus (3:23-38) in two columns of 28 lines in each column. Instead of transcribing the text by following the columns in succession, the scribe of 109 copied the genealogy by following the lines across the two columns. As a result, not only is almost everyone made the son of the wrong father, but, because the names apparently did not

[11] Ibid., 12.

[12] Ibid., 14,186-194.

> fill the last column of the exemplar, the name of God now stands within the list instead of at its close (it should end, of course, '...Adam, the son of God'). In this manuscript God is actually said to have been the son of Aram, and the source of the whole race is not God but Phares!"[13]

Some manuscript alterations were made intentionally. For example, the Gnostic Marcion removed from the book of Luke all Jewish references that would contradict Marcion's teachings. In *Harmony of the Gospels,* Tatian also attempted to unify the gospel writings while altering the text to support his ascetic views. These and many more adjustments were made as individuals and groups sought to clarify misunderstood writings, promote personal preferences, achieve fame through invention, or acquire monetary gain.

To improve accuracy, during the Byzantine period (AD 135-638) monks were given the task of reproducing Scripture. In monastic communities there was less commercial pressure, allowing individual monks to work alone in their cells. The result of this concerted effort was a massive number of copied biblical texts. In fact, apologist Josh McDowell states that there are more than 24,970 known Greek manuscripts of the New Testament. In comparison, the second largest significant writing of antiquity, Homer's *Iliad*, was only copied 643 times.[14]

The tremendous amount of available manuscripts, and fragments of manuscripts, enables us to be confident as to what the original autographs actually contained. Consider the following fictitious example:

> Autograph: Jack went up the hill to fetch a pale of water.
> Manuscript #1: Mack went up the hill to get a pale of water.
> Manuscript #2: Jack went over the hill to fetch a pale of water.
> Fragment #1*: [missing]* up the hill to fetch a pale *[missing]*
> Fragment #2: Jack went up *[illegible text]* pale of water.

Even with numerous human errors and missing information, in this example it is evident what the original author's writing, the autograph, was

---

[13] Metzger, *Text of New Testament*, 195.

[14] Josh McDowell. *The New Evidence that Demands a Verdict.* (Nashville: Thomas Nelson, 1999), 34.

meant to convey. This is why we should be encouraged by the plethora of manuscripts and fragments which have been preserved. We can be sure of what the original autographs said. Moreover, the way God preserved his Word for us was not some mystical process we cannot explain. He used hundreds of men and thousands of handwritten copies to preserve for us exactly what he intended to be revealed through the ages.

Historical Setting and the Need for Canon

The Jewish Diaspora, or Dispersion, began in BC 597 with the first of three Babylonian exiles, and lasted until AD 1948.[15] Spanning such a long time period, numerous political changes caused further dispersion of the Jewish people. As they became acclimated to new areas throughout the Roman Empire, the ancestral Hebrew language of the Jews was superseded by the Greek language, which was promoted by Alexander the Great during his conquests.[16] A significant by-product of this common language was that it would be a great benefit to evangelism after the coming of Christ.

By the death of Jesus in AD 33, the New Testament period offered a fertile landscape for the spread of new teachings. In addition to a common language throughout the empire, Greek influence also promoted logic and learning. Many Jews were well educated, adapted to the customs of their new societies, and became quite successful. Moreover, once a prominent Jew was converted he had the means to support the new movement. The spread of Christianity was even further accommodated by the Romans through the provision of better roads, general peace due to governmental control, and protection under civil laws.[17, 18]

---

15 Tim Dowley. *Baker Atlas of Christian History.* (Grand Rapids: Baker, 2002), 48.

16 The Septuagint, a Greek translation of the Hebrew Old Testament, was written between BC 285 and BC 130 so that these new "Hellenized" Jews could retain the teachings of their forefathers.

17 John Phillips. *Exploring the Scriptures: An Overview of the Bible from Genesis to Revelation.* (Grand Rapids: Kregel Publications, 2001), 168.

18 Justo L. Gonzalez. The Story of Christianity. Volume 1: The Early Church to the Dawn of the Reformation. (San Franciso: HarperCollins, 1984), 12.

According to the book of Acts, the early church was born when the Holy Spirit descended upon about 120 disciples as they gathered for the Feast of Pentecost. As Christians began to meet, first in homes and later in dedicated buildings, the Old Testament Scriptures would be read to a mostly illiterate congregation. Adding to this instruction, over a period of about thirty years Jesus' teachings were conveyed orally by his closest disciples, still without any written manuscripts.[19] As these teachers died, however, the church began to lose its direct source of the Lord's verbal revelation. Therefore, in order to preserve the integrity of his teaching the church began to recognize the importance of saving the writings of his ministry partners. And so began a journey toward establishing what writings should and should not be held as Scripture, a process referred to as canonization.

---

[19] Ewert, *Ancient Tablets*, 113.

Part 2: Canonization

Introduction

Since the earliest records of human society we have relied on evidence to distinguish fact from fiction. So, if there were simple proof of how we received the New Testament as it stands today, then there would be few writings on the subject and little debate as to its relevance in our lives. However, there is no evidence that proves, without question, the authority that Christians attribute to the modern New Testament.[20] While the books of the Old Testament are seldom questioned, the way in which the New Testament books were selected may cause some people to doubt that we have the correct writings and that none can be further added. This potential for doubting must therefore be addressed if Christians are to be strong in our faith and have the relationship with God through written revelation, the truth of which gives purpose and joy to our lives.

As with any other scientific or historical investigation, there must be a fundamental assumption or belief from which to construct and test theories or hypotheses. In this analysis the basis for examination will be that the New Testament would not exist if it were not for the life and teachings of one man, Jesus of Nazareth. The Word, as he is called in the book of John, is a fitting name because without Jesus there would be no written "Word" involving the New Testament. In fact, Nelson's Bible Dictionary states explicitly that "The New Testament presents the record of Jesus' life, teachings, death, and resurrection; a narrative of the beginning of the Christian church… It also contains the written teachings of Jesus' apostles and other early Christians who applied the principles of his teaching and redemptive work to their lives."[21] Even from secular sources it can be seen that Jesus' life sparked a flame of religiosity that to this day has been unmatched in fervor and in number of adherents. To believers, though, his life and ministry provided both example and meaning. He was the initiator of Christian thought, the perfection of human existence,

---

[20] G.E. Ladd. "Canon of the NT," in *The International Standard Bible Encyclopedia*, ed. Geoffrey W. Bromiley. (Grand Rapids: William B. Eerdmans Publishing, 1979), 601.
[21] Youngblood, *Bible Dictionary*, 187.

the incarnation of Almighty God, the conqueror of evil, and the Savior who would rescue humanity from eternal separation with its Creator.

With the advent of Christianity came a fervent passion for persons to change their lives drastically in order to be obedient to their Lord. Consequently, the Bible became a source of contention even among Christians themselves. Although all Christian denominations originated from the *early church*, referred to then as the *catholic* or *universal church*, understanding and application of biblical passages has led to many schisms throughout history. For example, one of the main convictions that sparked the Protestant Reformation in the 1500's was referred to as *sola Scriptura*, meaning "the Bible alone." Norman Geisler defines what Protestants mean by this phrase, explaining that "the Bible alone is the infallible written authority for faith and morals."[22] This is only one of many examples which could illustrate that the Bible is a book of controversy and intrigue. Therefore, confidence that we have a complete and final collection of biblical books is a matter of crucial importance to every believer. This chapter will explain the basic process by which books were selected for inclusion in the New Testament, and defend the position that it is complete.

Survey of Positions

Closed Canon

The term *testament* in both Hebrew and Greek meant settlement, treaty, or covenant. Of these definitions, *covenant* has particularly important connotations with regard to the Bible. The first half of the Bible is usually referred to as the Old Testament because it contains Scriptures pertaining to the Old Covenant relationship between God and his people, which was initiated by God through the Ten Commandments he gave to Moses at Mt. Sinai.[23] After Jesus entered human history, God's people entered into a new era in which our relationship to him falls under a new covenant. During

---

[22] Geisler, Norman L. and Ralph E. MacKenzie. *Roman Catholics and Evangelicals: Agreements and Differences.* (Grand Rapids: Baker Book House, 1995), 178.

[23] Youngblood, *Bible Dictionary*, 183.

the Passover supper on the night before his death the Lord encouraged his disciples with a glass of wine, symbolically proclaiming, "This cup is the new covenant [established by] my blood."[24] (Luke 22:20 NIV) All Scripture written from that point forward expounds upon what the New Covenant means, and we typically refer to these writings as the New Testament.

The Greek word *kanon*, or *canon* in English, stems from a Semitic word for reed. This description progressed to a measuring reed, and from there became rule, standard, or norm. Eventually the word referred to a list or table. D. A. Carson states that in the first three centuries of the early church, canon was defined as the "normative doctrinal and ethical content of Christian faith." He further states that by the fourth century canon was used to describe a list of Old Testament and New Testament books, and that today we use the term to describe a "closed collection of documents that constitute authoritative Scripture."[25] By *closed* we mean that the canon contains all written revelation which God intended to preserve for the church, so there are no additional writings to be considered as Scripture. Table 1 lists the closed New Testament canon in use today.[26]

Table 1. Books of the New Testament

GOSPELS	HISTORY	EPISTLES		APOCALYPSE
		Pauline	***General***	
Matthew	Acts	Romans	Hebrews	Revelation
Mark		1 Corinthians	James	
Luke		2 Corinthians	1 Peter	
John		Galations	2 Peter	
		Ephesians	1 John	
		Philippians	2 John	
		Colossians	3 John	
		1 Thessalonians	Jude	
		2 Thessalonians		
		1 Timothy		
		2 Timothy		
		Titus		
		Philemon		

---

[24] The KJV translation actually uses the term "new testament" here.

[25] D.A. Carson, Douglas J. Moo, and Leon Morris. *An Introduction to the New Testament.* (Grand Rapids: Zondervan, 1992), 487.

[26] McDowell, *Evidence that Demands a Verdict*, 25.

Open Canon

The way the church came about canonizing sixty-six books, particularly the twenty-seven New Testament books, has caused some to doubt the precision with which it was done. It is argued that there were many additional manuscripts available which were not included in the canon, but perhaps should have been. Furthermore, one may question why the church insists that modern writings may not be added.[27]

Following this line of reasoning, some scholars in recent years have argued for the inclusion of additional ancient writings such as the gospel accounts of Judas, Thomas, Philip, and Mary Magdalen. Moreover, if the canon is open then additional revelation from God may be available in more recent documents such as the Book of Mormon and the Koran.[28]

If there are no clear reasons with which to be confident that the canon is closed, then our belief system would seem to benefit from additional writings. After all, there are many aspects of our lives in which more is better. The Bible teaches us to be more righteous, more self-controlled, more peaceful, more patient, more forgiving, more loving, more active on behalf of others, more faithful, more obedient, more wise, and so on. With regard to the biblical canon, then, its importance to Christians would be neglected if there were instructions from God that we intentionally refused to receive.

Support for a Closed Canon

The greatest support for a closed New Testament canon is the method by which we came to recognize it as God's final and authoritative revelation. Although many writings were available, and additional texts have been discovered throughout the centuries, the method of canonization still

---

[27] Bart D. Ehrman. "Lost Scriptures: Books that Did Not Make It into the New Testament." (London: Oxford University Press, 2003) [on-line]; accessed 1 July 2010; available from http://www.bartdehrman.com/books/lost_scriptures.htm; Internet.

[28] James R. White. *Scripture Alone: Exploring the Bible's Accuracy, Authority, and Authenticity.* (Minneapolis, MN: BethanyHouse, 2004), 110.

remains a dependable process. As an appropriate introduction to the process of canonization, Bruce Metzger states the following:

> "Besides textual evidence derived from New Testament Greek manuscripts and from early versions, the textual critic has available numerous scriptural quotations included in the commentaries, sermons, and other treatises written by early Church Fathers. Indeed, so extensive are these citations that if all other sources for our knowledge of the text of the New Testament were destroyed, they would be sufficient alone for the reconstruction of practically the entire New Testament."[29]

Table 2. Church Fathers

NAME	DATE *(A.D.)*
Marcion	c. 160
Justin Martyr	d. 165
Tatian	c. 170
Irenaeus, Bishop of Lyons	d. 202
Clement of Alexandria	d. 212
Tertullian of Carthage	d. 220
Hippolytus of Rome	d. 235
Origen of Alexandria and Caesarea	d. 254
Cyprian, Bishop of Carthage	d. 258
Eusebius, Bishop of Caesarea	d. 340
Ambrosiaster of Rome	c. 350+
Hilary of Poitiers	d. 367
Lucifer of Calaris	d. 371
Athanasius, Bishop of Alexandria	d. 373
Ephraem the Syrian	d. 373
Gregory of Nazianzus in Cappadocia	d. 390
Gregory of Nyssa in Cappadocia	d. 394
Ambrose of Milan	d. 397
Didymus of Alexandria	d. 398
Pelagius	c. 400
Epiphanius, Bishop of Salamis	d. 403
Chrysostom, Bishop of Constantinople	d. 407
Rufinus of Aquileia	d. 410
Jerome	d. 420
Theodore of Mopsuestia in Cilicia	d. 428
Augustine, Bishop of Hippo	d. 430
Isidore of Pelusium	d. 435
Cyril of Alexandria	d. 444
Pseudo-Hieronymus	c. 500
Primasius, Bishop of Hadrumentum	d. 552

[29] Metzger, *Text of New Testament*, 86.

Table 2 lists the most influential Church Fathers, who are sometimes also referred to as Apostolic Fathers.[30] Although their own works were not considered to *be* Scripture, these men were instrumental in establishing which texts were worthy of inclusion in the canon.[31] In their writings, the fathers often quoted from certain manuscripts, thereby supporting the inclusion of those documents in the New Testament canon. These numerous quotations are tallied in Table 3.[32]

Table 3. Early Patristic Quotations of the New Testament

WRITER	GOSPELS	ACTS	EPISTLES *Pauline*	EPISTLES *General*	REVELATION	TOTALS
Justin Martyr	268	10	43	6	3	330
Irenaeus	1,038	194	499	23	65	1,819
Clement of Alexandria	1,017	44	1,127	207	11	2,406
Origen	9,231	349	7,778	399	165	17,922
Tertullian	3,822	502	2,609	120	205	7,258
Hippolytus	734	42	387	27	188	1,378
Eusebius	3,258	211	1,592	88	27	5,176
TOTALS	**19,368**	**1,352**	**14,035**	**870**	**664**	**36,289**

Coincidently, as the need for an official canon became apparent the advent of the codex provided a means to group the selected texts together. This idea caught on and many began to proclaim which "books" they thought should be included. The first canonical list was produced in AD 140 by Marcion. Believing that the god of the Old Testament was evil, and the god of the New Testament was good, he removed all books that referenced Old Testament Scripture. As a result, his canon only included ten of Paul's letters and an edited version of Luke.[33]

Refuting Marcion in AD 180, Irenaeus included the four Gospels. However, he distinguished each book as a separate account, relating them to four points on a compass, four covenants, or four living creatures. This understanding was contrary to the generally accepted view that the gospels were synoptic. Even so, his work was important in that he defended the inclusion of these narratives as part of God's written revelation to man.

---

[30] Ibid., 88.

[31] David Ewert. *From Ancient Tablets to Modern Translations: A General Introduction to the Bible.* (Grand Rapids: Zondervan, 1983), 118.

[32] McDowell, *Evidence that Demands a Verdict,* 43.

[33] Carson, Moo, and Morris. *An Introduction to the New Testament.* 492.

Yet another combatant for the developing canon was Tatian. In his *Diatessaron* of AD 160, he went beyond synopticism and combined the four Gospels into a single account.[34] Although it is evident that both heretical and orthodox Apostolic Fathers varied in their understanding of the apostles' writings, these few examples of early canonical criticisms demonstrate an increasing awareness that certain writings should be treated with greater respect than others.

The church quickly realized the need for an established process which would ensure accuracy and comprehensiveness in the official canon. Their mode of canonization is stated well by Geisler, "Canonicity is *determined* or established authoritatively by God; it is merely *discovered* by man."[35] The Church Fathers sought to discern which writings actually *were* God's revealed truth. According to the self-attesting words of 2 Peter 3:1-2, the Scriptures are given "so that you can remember the words previously spoken by the holy prophets and the command of our Lord and Savior *through your apostles*."[36]

The first, and most important, criterion used in the *discovering* of canonical writings was *apostolicity*. Tertullian stated, "We lay it down first of all that the Evangelical instrument has a*postles as authors*, upon whom this duty of promulgating the Gospel was laid by the Lord himself."[37] To be considered for inclusion, then, a work had to be received from an apostle or someone closely connected with an apostle.

The next stipulation was *catholicity*. The usage of a document needed to be applicable abroad. Although many of the writings included in the canon were addressed to specific churches, their contents were deemed useful for all churches.

Orthodoxy provided a third test. The teachings within a canonical writing were required to be complimentary to the traditional faith of the church. It was commonly held that Scripture and tradition helped to fashion one another, guided by God so that the resulting canon would be

---

[34] Ewert, *From Ancient Tablets to Modern Translations*, 121.

[35] Norman L. Geisler and William E. Nix. *A General Introduction to the Bible*. Revised and Expanded. (Chicago: Moody Press, 1986), 221.

[36] Unless otherwise specified, all Scripture quotations in this chapter are taken from the HCSB translation.

[37] Walter A. Elwell and Robert W. Yarbrough. *Encountering the New Testament: A Historical and Theological Survey*. (Grand Rapids: Baker Book House, 1998), 71.

precisely what he wanted to reveal about himself. Any notion of lost or late Scriptures would contradict God's sovereign oversight of revelation.[38]

The final requirement was *traditional usage.* Works that had been proven useful as standard teaching material were considered more inspired than others that had not been used extensively.[39]

Discovering which texts met these criteria happened in several ways. As previously mentioned, some were acclaimed through the writings of the Church Fathers. A second approach to recognition emanated from comparison of canonical lists or translations, such as *The Old Syriac, The Old Latin*, and *The Muratorian Canon.* Thirdly, councils were held in which many great scholars would concur on specific issues such as canonization.[40] Table 4 depicts the essence of consensus and timing for these various forms of confirmation.[41]

---

[38] White, *Scripture Alone*, 110.

[39] Harry Y. Gamble. *The New Testament Canon: Its Making and Meaning.* (Philadelphia: Fortress Press, 1985), 68-70.

[40] Geisler and Nix. *A General Introduction to the Bible*, 292.

[41] Ibid., 295.

Table 4. The New Testament Canon During the First Four Centuries

BOOK	INDIVIDUAL																	CANON					TRANS.			COUNCIL			
	Pseudo-Barnabas (c. 70-130)	Clement of Rome (c. 95-97)	Ignatius (c. 110)	Polycarp (c. 110-150)	Hermas (c. 115-140)	Didache (c. 120-150)	Papias (c. 130-140)	Irenaeus (c. 130-202)	Diognetus (c. 150)	Justin Martyr (c. 150-155)	Clement of Alexandria (c. 150-215)	Tertullian (c. 150-220)	Origen (c. 185-254)	Cyril of Jerusalem (c. 315-386)	Eusebius (c. 325-340)	Jerome (c. 340-420)	Augustine (c. 400)	Marcion (c. 140)	Muratorian (c. 170)	Apostolic (c. 300)	Cheltenham (c. 360)	Athanasius (367)	Tatian Diatessaron (c. 170)	Old Latin (c. 200)	Old Syriac (c. 400)	Nicea (c. 325-340)	Hippo (393)	Carthage (397)	Carthage (419)
Matt.	X	X		X	X	X		O		X	X	X	X	O	O	O	O		O	O	O	O	O	O	O	O	O	O	O
Mark	X			X	X			O		X	X	X	X	O	O	O	O		O	O	O	O	O	O	O	O	O	O	O
Luke	X			X		X		O		X	X	X	X	O	O	O	O	O	O	O	O	O	O	O	O	O	O	O	O
John		X		X			X	O		O	X	X	X	O	O	O	O		O	O	O	O	O	O	O	O	O	O	O
Acts				X	X			O		X	X	X	X	O	O	O	O		O	O	O	O		O	O	O	O	O	O
Rom.		X		X		X		O		X	O	X	X	O	O	O	O	O	O	O	O	O		O	O	O	O	O	O
I Cor.		O		X	X	X		O		X	O	X	X	O	O	O	O	O	O	O	O	O		O	O	O	O	O	O
II Cor.				X	X			O	X	X	O	X	X	O	O	O	O	O	O	O	O	O		O	O	O	O	O	O
Gal.				X				O	X	X	O	X	X	O	O	O	O	O	O	O	O	O		O	O	O	O	O	O
Eph.	X	X	X	X				O		X	X	X	X	O	O	O	O	O	O	O	O	O		O	O	O	O	O	O
Phil.			X	X	X			O			O	X	X	O	O	O	O	O	O	O	O	O		O	O	O	O	O	O
Col.			X	X				O	X	X	O	X	X	O	O	O	O	O	O	O	O	O		O	O	O	O	O	O
I Thes.			X	X	X	X		O		X	X	X	X	O	O	O	O	O	O	O	O	O		O	O	O	O	O	O
II Thes.			X	X				O		X	X	X	X	O	O	O	O	O	O	O	O	O		O	O	O	O	O	O
I Tim.		X		X	X	X		X			O	X	X	O	O	O	O		O	O	O	O		O	O	O	O	O	O
II Tim.	X				X			X				X	X	O	O	O	O		O	O	O	O		O	O	O	O	O	O
Titus	X	X						X	X		O	X	X	O	O	O	O		O	O	O	O		O	O	O	O	O	O
Philemon			X											O	O	O	O	O	O	O	O	O		O	O	O	O	O	O
Hebrews	X	X			X			X			O	X	?	O	O	O	O			O		O			O	O	O	O	O
James		X			X									O	?	O	O			O		O			O	?	O	O	O
I Peter	X			X	X			O		X	O	X	O	O	O	O	O			O	O	O			O	O	O	O	O
II Peter	X	X											?	O	?	O	O			O	?	O				?	O	O	O
I John				X	X			O			O	X		O	O	O	O		O	O	O	O		O	O	O	O	O	O
II John				X				X					?	O	?	O	O		O	O	?	O		O		?	O	O	O
III John													?	O	?	O	O		O	O	?	O		O		?	O	O	O
Jude								X			O	X		O	?	O	O		O	O		O		O		?	O	O	O
Rev.					X	X	O	O		X	O	X	O		O	O	O		O		O	O		O		O	O	O	O

X = citation or allusion, O = named as authentic, ? = named as disputed

The twenty-seven books in the modern New Testament were first presented as canon by Athanasius of Alexandria (AD 298-373) in his thirty-ninth Festal (Easter) Letter, written in AD 367. The eastern churches quickly accepted his list, and at the Council of Carthage in AD 397 the western churches also approved.[42]

Paul's letters were the first to circulate together and were therefore the first collected for consideration in the orthodox canon.[43] There are two basic theories as to how Paul's letters were collected. One supposes that over time a single church may have collected letters that were written to other churches. Another theory proposes that one person may have undertaken the task of collecting all the letters. Nevertheless, the Pauline writings were first to achieve canonical status.[44]

The Gospels were first referenced in 8:2 of the *Didache*, a writing of unknown origin used as a guide for worship around AD 125.[45] Another early reference to the Gospels was in chapter 66 of Justin's Apologia of AD 150. In it he states, "For the apostles, in the *memoirs composed by them, which are called Gospels*, have thus delivered unto us what was enjoined upon them."[46]

Five books of the New Testament canon were written by men who were not listed as apostles, but whose direct association with Jesus or an apostle earned them the authority necessary for inclusion. Mark was closely associated with Peter. Luke, who also wrote the book of Acts, was a close companion and personal physician to the Apostle Paul during many journeys. And, although debatable, both Jude and James were believed to be half-brothers of Jesus.

---

[42] Wayne Grudem. *Systematic Theology: An Introduction to Biblical Doctrine.* (Grand Rapids: Zondervan, 1994), 64.

[43] David N. Freedman. "Canon," in *The Anchor Bible Dictionary.* ed. Gary A. Herion, David F. Graf, and John David Pleins. (New York: Doubleday, 1992), 853.

[44] Ewert, *From Ancient Tablets to Modern Translations,* 120.

[45] Alexander Souter. *The Text and Canon of the New Testament.* Revised by C. S. C. Williams. (London: Gerald Duckworth, 1954), 147.

[46] Terry Jones. *The First Apology of Justin Martyr.* Catholic Community Forum [on-line]. Accessed 20 April 2006. Available from http://www.catholic-forum.com/Saints/stj29002.htm; Internet.

Hebrews may be the only exception to the rule of apostolic authority, as its author is not firmly identified. Some have reasoned that Paul was the author, but this has not been proven decisively. It is clear, though, that Hebrews was included in the canon because its contents appeared to be self-attesting of divine authorship. Whatever the origin, its authenticity had never been seriously questioned by the many who scrutinized all of the Christian writings.[47]

In summary, many writings during the New Testament period were inspired by the life and teachings of Jesus Christ. As Jesus' apostles died, the catholic church recognized a need for an accurate compilation of works to serve as an authority for every follower of Christ. Thus, the Church Fathers embarked on a developmental process that lasted almost 400 years, but finally resulted in the canon that is still used by Christians today.

Objections to a Closed Canon

The Invention of Canon

It may be argued that the idea of canonization was a man-made concept which God never intended. Without any original autographs, and no direct revelation from God to suggest any exclusions, the church alone determined to leave out many available manuscripts. The fundamental basis for this objection would be that there is no evidence to suggest God used a slow process of humans recognizing Scripture which He had already prepared for them.

The Need for Canon

At the end of Part 1 it was explained that the canon came about during a season of great expansion in the Christian faith. An opponent of the closed canon could argue that the church invented the canon as a desperate act of preservation, since Jesus' apostles and their oral teachings

---

[47] Grudem. *Systematic Theology*, 62.

were fading into the past. Similar to the charter for a corporation, the church needed to document its fundamental teachings or else it would also fade along with the apostles.

The Self-Proclaimed Authority of the Catholic Church

Some insist that the church developed the idea of canon in order to assert control over its parishioners. It is argued that the church leaders selected which books to include, and that they therefore only selected books that would support their teaching.

Response in Defense of a Closed Canon

Authority to write Scripture rested with the Apostles, not the entire church. Apostles were special messengers of Jesus, those to whom he delegated authority for certain tasks. These men were commissioned by him to be his witnesses throughout the world.[48] Using a few passages from our modern New Testament, we can see how the apostle and his mission are defined. Luke 24:46-49 records Jesus' words, "This is what is written: the Messiah would suffer and rise from the dead the third day, and repentance for forgiveness of sins would be proclaimed in His name to all the nations, beginning at Jerusalem. *You are witnesses of these things.* And look, *I am sending you what My Father promised.* As for you, stay in the city until *you are empowered from on high.*" Luke again records in Acts 1:8 that Jesus said "*you will receive power when the Holy Spirit has come upon you, and you will be My witnesses* in Jerusalem, in all Judea and Samaria, and to the ends of the earth."

According to Mark 3:16-19, the initial twelve men Jesus appointed as apostles were: Simon Peter, James and John (sons of Zebedee), Andrew, Philip, Bartholomew, Matthew, Thomas, James the son of Alphaeus, Thaddaeus, Simon the Zealot, and Judas Iscariot. After Judas' betrayal and death, Acts 1:23-26 records that he was replaced by Matthias. James,

---

48 Youngblood, *Bible Dictionary*, 91.

the brother of Jesus, and Paul based their apostleship on the fact that they had seen the risen Lord and were specifically commissioned by him. Peter affirms Paul's apostleship in 2 Peter 3:15-16, where he instructs his readers to "regard the patience of our Lord as an opportunity for salvation, just as our dear brother Paul, *according to the wisdom given to him*, has written to you. He speaks about these things in all his letters, in which there are some matters that are hard to understand. The untaught and unstable twist them to their own destruction, *as they also do with the rest of the Scriptures*." (CSB) Furthering the expansion of apostolic authority, Paul indicates in 1 Corinthians 15:5-8 that there were *many* more apostles than just the original twelve.

The *Apostolic Age* describes the period in which the apostles lived, which lasted from the day of Pentecost in AD 30 to AD 100 when John died. All books currently included in the New Testament were written during that time period, giving rise to a new form of teaching within the church.[49, 50]

The first churches received their instruction primarily through the preaching of the apostles, using Old Testament Scripture and what the apostles knew personally of Jesus' teaching.[51] Moreover, there was initially no great urgency for the written word because the apostles were still living, Jesus had confirmed the authority of the Septuagint, scrolls and codices were difficult to produce and were therefore very expensive, and the mostly illiterate congregations saw no need for additional Scripture to be written down.[52]

However, as Christianity spread rapidly throughout the empire the apostles could not physically be present in every church. Simultaneously, various persecutions resulted in the death of many apostles, thus jeopardizing the continuance of their authoritative instruction.[53] Of further concern was the rise of heretical teaching, that which directly contradicted

---

49 Youngblood, *Bible Dictionary*, 92.

50 F.F. Bruce, Philip Comfort, Carl F.H. Henry, and J.I. Packer. *The Origin of the Bible*. (Wheaton: Tyndale House, 2003), 9.

51 Carson, Moo, and Morris, *An Introduction to the New Testament*, 487.

52 Ewert, *From Ancient Tablets to Modern Translations*, 114.

53 Walter A. Elwell and Robert W. Yarbrough. *Encountering the New Testament: A Historical and Theological Survey*. (Grand Rapids: Baker Book House, 1998), 74.

orthodoxy. With the apostolic age fading into history, the church needed written revelation from God in order to refute heretics and to provide a standard of truth for everyday living.[54] Thus, they relied primarily upon apostolic authority in order to discern which books God had given to be canonized as Scripture.

The canon was therefore not invented by man, but rather it was given of God providentially at the proper time in history when it was needed most. With Jesus as its main subject the New Testament could only be written by those to whom he had given apostolic authority. And as those apostolic sources began to fade, the church realized the tremendous need to capture their teaching in written form. The closing of the canon therefore depended not upon the self-proclaimed authority of the church, but rather it depended upon the Christ-imposed authority of the apostles. When the physical presence of apostolic authors ended around AD 100, so too did the writing of new Scripture.

After years of evaluating manuscript evidence and determining a reliable process for canonization, the church discovered with confidence what Scriptures the Lord had providentially inspired and saved for us. The result was that in AD 397 the church formally recognized with certainty that our New Testament canon was complete.[55]

---

[54] Ewert, *From Ancient Tablets to Modern Translations*, 118.

[55] It should be noted that in the 1500's the Roman Catholic Church acknowledged as canonical additional books for inclusion in their Bible. Protestant denominations, however, do not accept these "Apocrypha" to be authentic and authoritative Scripture. For more detail regarding these extra-canonical books, see "What are the Apocrypha / Deuterocanonical books?" [online], accessed 20 October 2015; available from http://www.gotquestions.org/apocrypha-deuterocanonical.html

Question 2

What is Repentance?

Introduction

If you have attended church for very long at all, especially in the Bible belt of the Southeastern U.S., there is a scene which is probably quite familiar to you. Imagine that your pastor is leading the congregation through a study of Jesus' teachings in the Sermon on the Mount. On this particular Sunday he has exhorted from Matthew 5:14-16 that "you are the light of the world… Let your light shine before others, so that they may see your good works and give glory to your Father who is in heaven."[56] He says that once you accept Jesus as your Savior there is a dramatic change in your actions. As he walks across the platform, he begins to explain that you are not only to have faith but also that you must *repent.* Suddenly, he turns 180 degrees and walks in the opposite direction. This, he says, illustrates what happens when you repent. You begin to walk in a different direction. Your life looks completely different as a Christian than it did prior to your conversion, and God is glorified when others see your new way of living.

Now imagine that a few Sundays go by and the pastor, progressing through Jesus' sermon, reaches Matthew 6:1-6. "Beware of practicing your righteousness before other people in order to be seen by them." The

---

[56] Unless otherwise specified, all Scripture quotations in this chapter are taken from the ESV translation.

pastor warns that Christians are not to be hypocrites, living a life of piety so that others may see. Being a studious person, you review notes from the previous sermon in which Christians were *commended* for being mindful of how their actions will appear to others. So, what are you to do? Do you glorify God with righteous living, or do you pretend that you are no different than anyone else and hide any righteous actions?

The answer lies in what motivates your actions. Consider, for example, how a wife does not appreciate the husband who only buys her flowers in order to get something he wants in return, or in a feeble attempt to make up for something foolish he has done. Rather, she appreciates the spontaneous gift that is the result of his love for her without care of how he may benefit. Love is his motivation, which can be seen by the good gesture of buying flowers. The flowers without love, however, would be pointless and simply remind the wife of her husband's lack of love. Similarly, the good works done by a Christian must be the result of a transformation within. The part of this inward transformation that you and I are held accountable for is what the Bible calls *repentance*.

The Problem of Sin

We often focus almost entirely on outward actions and neglect to consider what should motivate good works. We find ourselves struggling with a particular bad habit, and seek to correct the behavior because "that's not the kind of thing a Christian ought to do." Time and time again we attempt to make a positive change in our lives, only to either fail or to realize in the end that we were just trying to please people.

Your bad actions are not your problem. Rather, bad actions are *symptoms* of the real problem. And it is through *repentance* that you can deal with your real problem, which is the root cause of symptoms such as anxiety, lust, adultery, drunkenness, all kinds of addictions, foul speech, anger, and pride – just to name a few. In fact, the most significant difference between biblical counseling and traditional psychiatric care is the identification of a single root cause for every problem that a person encounters in life. This root cause is labeled in the Bible as sin, and it is manifested in one of two ways.

First, every created thing – you, me, all other people, the natural world itself – has been damaged by the introduction of sin in the Garden of Eden.[57] We tend to quickly move from Adam and Eve's disobedience to the subsequent curse they brought upon the world, which we term the "fall of man."[58] It is crucial, however, to contemplate what really happened with their disobedience. God had made covenant promises to them, based upon their willingness to worship him through obedience to his command. When they ate of the tree, their disobedience was more than just a simple *mistake*. In that one act they turned their allegiance, or their worship, from God to themselves. Rather than relying solely on the provision of their Creator, they determined to get for themselves something other than what he had provided. Adam and Eve wanted to be "like God," in essence setting themselves in the position of the one true God.[59]

Furthermore, sin is not only defined as disobedience toward God, but it is also anything that opposes his character. Because he is the giver of life, then, to turn away from him must result in the opposite of life – death. Therefore, the introduction of sin into the human race was a welcoming of opposition to God, a separation from God, an act of self-worship rather than God-worship, and the natural consequence could only be death. Though they thought they could be gods themselves, Adam and Eve could not sustain even their own lives. Of further consequence, God removed these death-bound humans from his "good" creation in Eden and placed them in an environment which suited their fate. Even to this day, all around us we see a world that is dying and decaying just as we are.[60]

The result of man's rebellion toward God has had far reaching effects upon every person. Death, natural disasters, harmful accidents, as well as both physical and mental illnesses occur because we live in a fallen world. When dealing with these situations, biblical counseling recognizes that modern secular methods or medications may need to be prescribed.

---

[57] The Apostle Paul wrote that "creation was subjected to frustration" and will someday be "liberated from its bondage to decay." (Romans 8:19-22) Moreover, he says that we who inhabit the earth are inherently corrupt and that "those controlled by the sinful nature cannot please God." (Romans 8:8)

[58] See Genesis 3 and Romans 5:18.

[59] See Genesis 3:4.

[60] See Genesis 3:17-19 and Romans 8:22.

But to deal adequately with the various kinds of trauma associated with uncontrollable events and circumstances, a person needs more than just something to temporarily numb the pain. Only God's Word can sufficiently restore hope, because ultimately the only thing worthy of our hope is God himself. No human actions, medical treatments, or rehabilitation programs can ever be as dependable as our Heavenly Father in helping us to cope with the fallen world and its effects upon our lives.

The second way sin deserves blame is by its direct compulsion of our wills, which causes us to make poor decisions and thereby suffer unpleasant consequences. Every person's will is by nature self-serving. In the Bible, the heart is often used to describe our will or desires.[61] One of many examples can be found in Jeremiah 17:9. "The heart is deceitful above all things, and desperately sick; who can understand it?"[62]

Today we continue to use the heart as a metaphoric residing place of our will, desire, longing, and deepest emotions. For example, the box of chocolates you buy for someone on Valentine's Day is shaped like a heart. When you see a carving on a tree that says "Jimmy + Suzie," it usually is encompassed by a heart. And, what do little girls write all over their school notebooks? "I ♥ so-and-so." Many years ago a man who was both my boss and a mentor told me, "You can do anything you want to in life if you'll put your heart into it." It's rather obvious in all these examples that the literal, physical, blood-pumping heart of a human's body is not in view. Rather, what is being called the heart is the center of our personality, involving intuition, feeling, emotion, and desire. Using the terms "heart" and "head" simply help us to distinguish our will from our intellect. For example, you may know in your head that an apple is a better snack than a piece of chocolate pie. But you choose the pie because in your heart, or with your will, you desire it more than the apple. Regardless of which choice is most logical, you want what you want. Thus, we understand

---

[61] In Psalm 14:1-3, David laments that all men are corrupt in their hearts. And in Psalm 51:5 he emphasizes his own wretchedness.

[62] See also James 1:14-15, which states that "each person is tempted when he is lured and enticed by his own desire. Then desire when it has conceived gives birth to sin, and sin when it is fully grown brings forth death."

the contrast between logic and desire by using the metaphoric imagery of head and heart.[63]

Because of sin's compelling control over a person's heart, the result may be wrong behavior such as substance abuse, lying, steeling, abusive language, physical abuse, impatience, perfectionism, smoking, and so forth. It's important to remember, however, that these wrong behaviors are symptoms, not causes. Though drunkenness may contribute to a bad marriage, it is not the root cause since it is itself a symptom of a sin problem in the person's heart. In order for a person to discontinue his or her bad actions, or outward behavior, an inward change of heart must take place.

Consider this example. As an auto mechanic many years ago I found great humor in fixing problems that other mechanics or do-it-yourselfers had made worse by simply "throwing parts" at a problem. Many times I would receive an older car that had very little power at high speeds, yet was "guzzling" gasoline. I would raise the hood and see new high-performance spark plug wires and the most expensive spark plugs on the market. Sometimes the owner had installed a grossly overpriced high-performance air filter, and even used a fuel additive to clean out the injectors. But all those parts did not fix the problem, which was the restricted fuel filter hidden inside the frame underneath the car. With the best of intentions, someone did all he could think of to correct the symptom but never discovered the root cause of his problem. Once the root cause was dealt with, the problem was overcome.

Christians are called to counsel one another with biblical wisdom in order to combat the effects of being sinners in a sin-stricken world. And as we seek to counsel one another biblically, there is one main issue to deal with in any situation. This one root cause is sin. Every problem a person struggles with is either due to the fact that we are living in a fallen (sinful) world, or there is a heart issue in which sin has control of a person's desires. Therefore, in order to be relieved of his or her problem a person must somehow remove or overcome sin.

---

[63] Merriam-Webster's online dictionary provides one meaning of *head* as "a person's mental ability; mind or intellect." The same dictionary states that in one sense "the *heart* is thought of as the place where emotions are felt."

Overcoming Sin

The Bible tells us that someday Christ will restore the earth to its original sinless state.[64] Until then, we cannot *remove* sin from around us, nor can we *remove* the sin nature inside us. However, even in this evil age we can *overcome* sin in our hearts. This is the storyline of the entire Bible. God is redeeming for himself a group of people who will be His image-bearers for all of eternity.[65] And in order to bear God's image, His glory in us cannot be tarnished by sin.[66] Therefore, He has made a way for us to be freed from sin's bondage right now.

Jesus Christ was the perfect sacrifice for all human sins – past, present, and future. By being fully human, while also remaining fully God, Jesus took your place on the cross as a substitute for the death penalty you owe, and He then demonstrated divine authority over death by being raised from the tomb.[67] The Bible proclaims the good news that salvation from sin is available to you. "If you confess with your mouth Jesus as Lord, and believe in your heart that God raised Him from the dead, you will be saved." (Romans 10:9 NASB) This "belief" we commonly call faith. And the confessing of "Jesus as Lord" is the result of a crucial transformation from self-worship to Savior-worship, a shifting of allegiance defined biblically as *repentance.*[68]

As we recognize our own sin*ful*ness, we realize the necessity of Jesus' sin*less*ness. He was not just a good moral example for us to follow. He was the perfectly obedient son which you and I cannot be. Jesus is the only man of whom God could rightly say, "This is my beloved son in whom

---

[64] We see in 2 Peter 3:13 that "according to his promise we are waiting for new heavens and a new earth in which righteousness dwells."

[65] See Genesis 1:26 for our purpose as God's image-bearers.

[66] Romans 3:23 says that "all have sinned and fall short of the glory of God."

[67] See Romans 5:6-11 for a detailed description of Jesus' substitutionary work.

[68] See Matthew 3:6, in which the Messiah's forerunner preached that men must repent because Jesus' kingdom was near. Jesus also preached the same message from the beginning of his earthly ministry, as recorded in Matthew 4:17, "Repent, for the kingdom of heaven is at hand." Thus, in Jesus' kingdom the consequences of *The Fall* would be reversed just as the root cause of man's fallenness would be reversed through the act of repentance.

I am well-pleased."[69] (Matthew 3:17 NASB) We can only be God's children by being joined to his legitimate Son, and this is done through faith.[70] This faith is brought about by a person seeing his or her need of it, which is an act of repentance. In this way, "by the one man's [Jesus] obedience the many will be made righteous." (Romans 5:19) This repentance, then, is the undoing of *The Fall.*

Puritan pastor Thomas Watson wrote, "I am sure that repentance is of such importance that there is no being saved without it."[71] In fact, repentance is so important that it was a main theme throughout the ministry of our Lord Jesus. The first word of His first recorded sermon was, "Repent!" (Matthew 4:17) And the last command He gave in His farewell message to the disciples was that "repentance should be preached" in His name. (Luke 24:47) From beginning to end, throughout His ministry Jesus emphasized the need for sinners to repent. Evidently, then, the way for Jesus' victory over sin to be applied to you and me is through repentance.

The Function of Repentance

"All have sinned and fall short of the glory of God," and "the wages of sin is death, but the free gift of God is eternal life in Christ Jesus our Lord." (Romans 3:23, 6:23) To be "in Christ" means that Jesus is your substitute in death, and He is your hope for resurrection. But how do you appropriate His atonement for your sin? What must you do to be saved, not only from the temporary trials of today but more importantly from the eternal fiery ordeal of tomorrow? You must die!

---

[69] See also the Transfiguration recorded in Luke 9:35, in which God the Father says, "This is my Son, my Chosen One; listen to him!"

[70] See Hebrews 3:6, which states that "Christ is faithful over God's house as a son. And we are his house if indeed we hold fast our confidence and our boasting in our hope." See also Romans 8:17.

[71] Thomas Watson, *The Doctrine of Repentance* (East Peoria, IL: Versa Press, 2009), 12. See also Thomas Watson, "The Doctrine of Repentance" [on-line], accessed 10 September 2015; available from http://www.gracegems.org/Watson/repentance.htm; Internet.

> [3] Do you not know that all of us who have been baptized into Christ Jesus were baptized into his death? [4] We were buried therefore with him by baptism into death, in order that, just as Christ was raised from the dead by the glory of the Father, we too might walk in newness of life. [5] For if we have been united with him in a death like his, we shall certainly be united with him in a resurrection like his. [6] We know that our old self was crucified with him in order that the body of sin might be brought to nothing, so that we would no longer be enslaved to sin. [7] For one who has died has been set free from sin. (Romans 6:3-7)

Baptism represents man's identification with Christ's death, burial, and resurrection. The above passage states affirmatively that the natural man must die, as symbolized in baptism, in order to remedy his corrupt, sinful nature. Baptism by immersion therefore presents a clear picture that one is dying to self, and being made alive with Christ. Going under the water represents the person's desire that his natural man be put to death, as Christ's body was also buried. Coming up out of the water is symbolic of being raised into eternal life, as Christ also was raised. This *believer's baptism,* accomplished only by a person capable of moral responsibility, is both an identification of what Christ has done for him and an act of obedience to the commands of Christ.[72] This obedience comes about by the changing of the mind with regard to one's own sin. The convert desires to put to death his old, sinful nature, and seek a new life of Christlikeness instead.[73]

---

[72] See Matthew 3:13-17, in which Jesus' cousin John baptized him. In following Jesus, his disciples today also follow his example by being baptized in a similar manner as he was. See also Matthew 28:18-20, which is often called *The Great Commission*. In it Jesus commanded Christians to proclaim the good news (gospel) of salvation throughout the world and to baptize any who would turn from their sin to follow Christ.

[73] See Ephesians 4:22-24 for the "put off" and "put on" concept. Every believer needs to stop certain actions and attitudes which are sinful, and replace them with holy ones. This process is called sanctification, and is the overarching goal of

This change of mind is part of what the Bible defines as repentance. Therefore, the way of death for God's children is through repentance rather than a literal, physical death.[74] And once the old nature is dead, the new Christian has the assurance of living eternally under the gracious control of Jesus Christ.[75] Hence, repentance is *dying in order that you may live.*[76]

The Essence of Repentance

Repentance in Scripture

Repentance is described frequently in the New Testament, and is a term used in conjunction with various concepts. In the gospels, for example, Mark describes each aspect of the conversion process as being closely connected with repentance. Some of these connections involve faith, forgiveness, entrance to the Kingdom, and the message to be proclaimed by Jesus' disciples.[77] The whole life of a believer, then, involves repentance.

The term repentance also occurs alongside other important action verbs, in formulas with definitive results. Consider the following:

> Repent and pray to receive forgiveness of a sinful heart. (Acts 8:22)
> Repent and be baptized to receive the Holy Spirit. (Acts 2:38)
> Repent and turn in order to do appropriate deeds. (Acts 26:20)

---

biblical counseling. See also Colossians 3:1-17 for a comprehensive list of actions and attitudes to "put on."

[74] See Romans 6:5 which says, "For if we have been united with him in a death like his, we shall certainly be united with him in a resurrection like his."

[75] See Philippians 1:27-28 in which Paul says to "let your manner of life be worthy of the gospel of Christ… and not frightened in anything by your opponents. This is a clear sign to them of their destruction, but of your salvation, and that from God."

[76] The original title of this paper was *Dying to Live: The Nature and Necessity of Biblical Repentance.*

[77] J. Lunde, *Repentance*, in *Dictionary of Jesus and the Gospels*, ed. Joel B. Green, Scot McKnight, I. Howard Marshall (Downers Grove, IL: Intervarsity Press, 1992), 672. See also Mark 1:4, 1:15, and 6:12.

Repent and do good in order to be a continued witness. (Rev. 2:5)

Repent and return for the removal of sins. (Acts 3:19)

These formulas indicate that repentance is to be *done* in coordination with prayer, baptism, reoriented worship, and good deeds. Furthermore, repentance is a key ingredient in *receiving* forgiveness, the Holy Spirit, the ability to do good and thereby witnessing to Christ, and it is necessary for acquittal from condemnation.

It should be noted that the "doing good" of Revelation 2:5 was the result of repentant "turning" in Acts 26:20. This refutes the idea that good works may be done first, and are then the wellspring from which come all the benefits listed above. Good works are not "instruments of healing."[78] On the contrary, they are the *result* of healing. Repentance comes first, and then a person will "bear fruit in keeping with [it]."[79]

The earliest disciples commanded repentance as the proper response to the gospel message.[80] Following a repentant response to the gospel were such actions as baptism.[81] Therefore, the Great Commission given by Jesus himself in Matthew 28:18-20 rests upon a foundation of repentance by which three actions are commanded. First, disciples are to be *made*, corresponding to the "turn/return" concept in Acts 26:20 and 3:19. Second, disciples are to be *baptized*, as echoed in Acts 2:38. And third, disciples are to be taught *obedience*, which relates to the "do good" command of Revelation 2:5.

So then, the Great Commission instructs current disciples to use as evangelistic tools four of the five formulas noted earlier in our survey of New Testament usage for the term *repent.* Notice that the only formula left

---

[78] Marcellino D'Ambrosio, *Exploring the Catholic Church: An Introduction to Catholic Teaching and Practice* (Cincinnati, OH: St. Anthony Messenger Press, 2001), 116.

[79] As recorded in Matthew 3:8, John the Baptist prepared the way for Jesus' earthly ministry by declaring that true repentance results in a change in outward behavior. However, he chastised the religious leaders harshly for only *pretending* to be repentant. He also preached in 3:10 that Jesus was soon coming to separate the *genuinely* repentant from those whose conversions were false.

[80] See Mark 6:12.

[81] See Acts 2:38.

out of the Great Commission is *repentance with prayer*, which we saw in Acts 8:22. It is likely that prayer is left out of Jesus' command so that there may be no confusion as to whose prayer is connected with repentance in an individual. The commission involves actions which are clearly prescribed to existing believers. The prayer of repentance, however, is a private matter to be done by an unbeliever upon hearing the gospel message. This prayer cannot be performed by, or made more effective by, other people.[82]

In addition to the Great Commission and the formulas previously mentioned, the word *repent* also occurs alongside other important action verbs. It is used in conjunction with such words as: believe, return, obey, turn, be zealous, and glorify God.[83] Moreover, it is clearly stated in numerous passages that repentance is necessary to avoid exile from the kingdom, which involves judgment and punishment for sin.[84] In summary, then, the New Testament ties repentance directly to conversion, to many subsequent acts in a believer's life, and to the hope we have for an eternal future in the Kingdom of Christ.

Components of Repentance

Thomas Watson described the components of repentance as: sight of sin, sorrow for sin, confession of sin, shame for sin, hatred for sin, and turning from sin.[85] Of these descriptions, the one to be dealt with first is perhaps the most illusively misunderstood – sorrow.

Sorrow. We can all picture a mother telling her child to say he is sorry, whether or not he actually means it. False sorrow is agreeable to sinful men because it is free of guilt, whereas godly sorrow properly assesses the high cost of guilt. Watson asserted that godly sorrow "must be as great as for

---

[82] The concept of repentance being an individual matter should not be confused with chapter four, in which it is argued that believers are to pray for God to act in bringing about repentance in a person so that he may grant the person eternal life. The point in the current chapter is that a person cannot directly accomplish repentance on behalf of someone else.

[83] See Mark 1:15, Acts 3:19, Rev. 3:3, 2:5, Acts 26:20, Rev. 3:19, 16:9.

[84] See Luke 13:3-5, 16:30, Acts 17:30, Rev. 2:5, 2:16, 2:21-22, 3:3.

[85] Watson, *Repentance*, 18.

any worldly loss."[86] He refers to Zechariah 12:10, in which God said "when they look on me, on him whom they have pierced, they shall mourn for him, as one mourns for an only child, and weep bitterly over him, as one weeps over a firstborn." This verse recognizes the agony of the Suffering Servant in taking upon himself the penalty we deserve.[87] Today most of us complain of any minor injustice done toward us as if it were a great and awful atrocity. Yet who of us has suffered as Christ did, and who of us has suffered as undeservedly as He did. With genuine repentance, so great is our sorrow over the death of Christ on our behalf that nothing else hurts as much. Certainly we detest the sin that drove the nails upon the cross, and we loath the fact that we continually drive them anew. As Watson put it, our sorrow is only sufficient "when the love of sin is purged out."[88]

This biblical concept of repentance, which involves great sorrow for sin, is not a popular notion today in society or in religion. Some even blatantly teach the opposite, saying such things as, "sorrow that leads to personal transformation isn't an emotion; it's a matter of decision."[89] On the contrary, as we saw in Zechariah's description of sorrow, it involves an emotional feeling similar to losing one's own child.

Sorrow is the primary motivation behind true repentance. Some teach that "God will accept whatever motivation we're able to come up with, even if it's not quite perfect yet… He rejoices in any movement in His direction."[90] But Jesus sternly warned against superficial appearances of piety, emphasizing that God sees "what is done in secret." (Matthew 6:16-18) Furthermore, such statements limit God's own initiative in salvation. Those whom He calls will certainly respond in repentance and faith.[91] Because God is the active agent in saving men, there is no middle ground

---

[86] Ibid, 23.

[87] See Isaiah 53 for the prophecy of Jesus crucifixion, describing Him as God's Suffering Servant.

[88] Watson, *Repentance*, 24.

[89] D'Ambrosio, *Catholic Church*, 112.

[90] Ibid, 114.

[91] See John 6:37. Also, God's sovereign election is the security of hope we have that "neither death nor life, nor angels nor rulers, nor things present nor things to come, nor powers, nor height nor depth, nor anything else in all creation, will be able to separate us from the love of God in Christ Jesus our Lord." (Rom. 8:38-39)

or wavering with uncertainty in His activity. God knows what He desires to do, and He does it. Any wavering in repentance is solely the fault of man. Thus, a person either repents because he is saved, or the person is unrepentant because he is not yet saved. When God saves a person, there is a complete transformation of the heart. There is no such thing as *almost* repenting, or *partially* repenting.

The vehicle by which God brings a person to repentance is sorrow. Through God's Word, specifically the gospel message, God works in the hearts of those whom He calls so that they are sorrowful to the point of repentance. For example, the Apostle Paul described the response of a letter he had written to the Corinthian church. He expressed gladness that the harsh letter "grieved [them] into repenting." (2 Corinthians 7:9) He went on to say that "godly grief produces a repentance that leads to salvation without regret, whereas worldly grief produces death." In other words, godly grief or sorrow leads to repentance and worldly grief leads only to remorse.[92]

Turning from sin. This calls into question the order of things – which comes first, the chicken or the egg. In this case, is salvation or repentance first? So far we have described repentance as being first (only briefly mentioning the reverse), and from our human perspective that is an acceptable viewpoint. However, from God's perspective the chicken comes before the egg – or, salvation before repentance. This is to say that God determined before creating the world whom He would save and whom He would not.[93] Since God foreknows His elect, He will move them to repentant faith at the appropriate time.[94] The beginning of the process of salvation, from a human standpoint, is called *regeneration*. God changes the heart of a person so that despite its corrupt, sinful nature the person is able to truly repent. Peter Jeffrey reminds us that regeneration is being

[92] Colin G. Kruse, *2 Corinthians*, in vol. 8 of *The Tyndale New Testament Commentaries*, ed. Leon Morris (Downers Grove, IL: Intervarsity Press, 1988), 145. See also other examples of godly grief involving David (2 Sam. 12:13), Peter (Mk 14:72), and Paul (Acts 9:1-22).

[93] Romans 9:15-21 declares that for God's own purposes He will have mercy on whomever He chooses.

[94] Romans 8:29-30 describes the process by which God brings His elect into the fullness of His image.

spiritually reborn in order that we may be able to repent and believe in the gospel.[95] Rebirth was also the analogy Jesus used with Nicodemus. He said that one must be "born again" to enter the kingdom of God.[96]

Repentance involves not only turning *from* sin, but also turning *to* God.[97] A man can easily assent to making lifestyle changes if he sees personal benefit in doing so. That is like taking different steps in the same direction. But the man who repents will turn completely around and head in a new direction. His sin, an "attitude of rebellion against the love and care and righteous authority of God," has been overcome so that he is no longer under its control.[98]

Regarding the components of repentance, your pastor's illustration of turning 180 degrees is absolutely correct. But this action, as previously demonstrated, must be motivated by godly sorrow. At this point we can see that true repentance is a very hard thing. Indeed, there are many hindrances which prevent a person from repenting. Next, we shall consider some of these hindrances.

Hindrances to Repentance

Apparent Goodness

A person who does not know he is sick will not take the medicine necessary for his cure.[99] This is the case of many sinners who think that they are basically good and undeserving of God's wrath. Rather than fleeing to the cross for forgiveness, this person blindly hopes that on judgment day his Maker will care nothing about some *minor* flaws. This man only compares his goodness with the wickedness of the world around him. He is blinded by the sinful state of all creation, so that he does not

---

[95] Peter Jeffrey, *Bitesize Theology* (Darlington, England: Evangelical Press, 2000), 54.

[96] See John 3:5-7.

[97] See Acts 3:19, where both aspects of repentance are described.

[98] Jeffrey, *Theology*, 57. See also Romans 6:18.

[99] Watson, *Repentance*, 99.

even know that his illness is terminal.[100] In response to man's tendency to compare his goodness with that of other sinners, Jesus said clearly that "unless you repent you will all likewise perish." (Luke 13:3)

Not only is this man deceived into thinking he is not so bad, but he also has a restricted view of God's mercy – that there will be no judgment. Often the gospel is preached as if salvation were already attained for everyone, with no response necessary by individuals. It is perceived that God will surely be merciful, subjecting only the worst of us to judgment and hellfire. Waving John 3:16 as his banner of universal forgiveness, this person does not recognize the danger of his condition.

> "How much worse punishment, do you think, will be deserved by the one who has spurned the Son of God, and has profaned the blood of the covenant by which he was sanctified, and has outraged the Spirit of grace? For we know him who said, 'Vengeance is mine; I will repay.' And again, 'The Lord will judge his people.' It is a fearful thing to fall into the hands of the living God." (Hebrews 10:29-31)

A further misconception regarding man's goodness is that God will always be patient with us. As Watson puts it, however, "forbearance does not excuse payment." He goes on to illustrate that "the longer God's arrow is drawing the deeper it will wound."[101] "For [God] says, 'In a favorable time I listened to you, and in a day of salvation I have helped you.' Behold, now is the favorable time; behold, now is the day of salvation." (2 Corinthians 6:2)

Good Works

It is common for an unbeliever to see no need of repentance because his actions are seemingly good in comparison with those around him.

---

[100] Recorded in John 14:17, Jesus said that spiritual blindness is the natural state of the world and that only by the Holy Spirit may we come to know the truth.

[101] Watson, *Repentance*, 104.

C. S. Lewis even suggests that humans are not completely depraved because, whether Christian or not, we still have the ability to do *some* good. While certain aspects of his position are debatable, his point is beneficial in discussing false repentance. As Lewis sees it, mankind is not completely depraved because "experience shows us much goodness in human nature."[102] This is a helpful reminder that God does still accomplish good even with the existence of evil. Particularly, though, we are reminded that unbelievers are capable of doing deeds which *appear* to be good. Otherwise, Jesus would not have reminded us that "the gate is small and the way is narrow that leads to life, and there are few who find it." (Matthew 7:14)

There are many people who do very good things, and generally live upstanding lives without doing harm to anyone else. However, unless Jesus lied many of these people are following a false hope to destruction. Pleasing man by good works is the broad way, whereas pleasing God by repenting unto Christ is the narrow way that few will find. Placing one's trust in his or her good works, rather than in the work of Christ, is a hindrance which may prevent that person from repenting.

Pious Acts

Furthering the concept of false repentance is the idea that certain "expressions of repentance help break our attachments to sin."[103] These expressions may involve praying, fasting, giving to charity, penitential days, or confession to another human being.[104] Again, this common teaching is actually the opposite of what Scripture asserts.

A very common theme in the gospels was Jesus' insistence that in the New Covenant the Law is fulfilled by God within the hearts of His people. Charles Spurgeon once preached that "this great blessing of pardoned sin is always connected with the renewal of the heart. It is not given *because* of the change of heart, but it is always given *with* the change of heart."[105] He drew this truth from Jeremiah 31:33, in which God said of His Law

[102] C. S. Lewis. *The Problem of Pain* (New York, NY: HarperCollins, 1996), 61.
[103] D'Ambrosio, *Catholic Church*, 116.
[104] Ibid, 116-120.
[105] Charles Spurgeon, "The Law Written on the Heart." *JBC* 12 (1994): 25.

that He would "write it in [our] hearts." And in Matthew 6:1, Jesus said to "beware of practicing your righteousness before other people in order to be seen by them, for then you will have no reward from your Father who is in heaven." This warning coincides well with His other teaching that one cannot please God by actions that do not stem from a repentant heart.[106] The biblical evidence, then, asserts that heart change only comes from God and that pious acts do not make one righteous.

Repentance is Too Easy

Many people wrongly think that salvation is attained simply by reciting certain words in a prayer, or by walking the aisle at a corporate worship gathering.[107] This misperception comes from a narrow reading of 1 John 1:9. "If we confess our sins, he is faithful and just to forgive us our sins and to cleanse us from all unrighteousness." The confession of sin here is more than simply listing a few sinful actions or attitudes that come to mind, and then reciting what has come to be known as the "sinner's prayer."

Looking still at chapter 1 of 1 John, consider the weight of verse six. "If we say we have fellowship with him while we walk in darkness, we lie and do not practice the truth." John's point is that true confession of sin involves a change in how we view ourselves, which then results in changed behavior. Otherwise, as verse eight reads, "we deceive ourselves and the truth is not in us." John is tying outward evidence with inward repentance. True confession always comes from the heart, with a changing of the will so that what a person says with his mouth corresponds with what he actually does with his actions. Just as pious acts do not save a person, neither does an act of prayer if it does not come from a repentant heart.

When a man perceives something to be easy, his attitude tends to be one of laziness. Thinking repentance is a simple act of man, with no miraculous working of God required to bring it about, the man sees no urgency to get on with it. It seems that he would "rather go sleeping to hell than weeping to heaven."[108]

---

[106] See also Matthew 6:2-5, 16-18.

[107] Watson, *Repentance*, 99.

[108] Ibid, 101.

Repentance is Too Hard

Another hindrance to repentance is the recognition that it is too hard. This is indeed a very true assessment, as genuine repentance of sin cannot be achieved by the natural man. His heart is "desperately wicked," loving sin more than God. (Jeremiah 17:9 KJV)

The good news is that God does for us what we cannot do for ourselves. Saving faith from a repenting heart is something we cannot generate for ourselves. "With man this is impossible, but with God all things are possible." (Matthew 19:26) Thankfully, the Holy Spirit regenerates a man's heart so that rather than loving sin he hates it.[109] This turning from loving wickedness to loving holiness is the reversal of what happened during *The Fall* in the Garden of Eden. God's plan is simple; repentance is the correction of misdirected worship. Rather than trying to do the impossible alone, we can trust God to do what we cannot do. "Return to the LORD your God, for he is gracious and merciful, slow to anger, and abounding in steadfast love." (Joel 2:13)

Undesirable Consequences

Absence of joy. It may seem that turning away from oneself, despising the sinfulness of your very being, would cause continual misery and remove all joy. This is another deception of sin. In actuality, true joy can only be found in Christ. In his kingdom the Christian will experience "righteousness and peace and joy in the Holy Spirit." (Romans 14:17) Repentance "does not crucify, but clarify our joy."[110]

Loss of worldly delights. The New Testament Scriptures, and other documents of historic record, tell us of many who have suffered great loss by claiming to be Christian. Jesus made clear in his teaching that his followers may not enjoy the comforts of this world, but that they should focus on accumulating "treasure in heaven" rather than on earth. (Luke

[109] In his conversation with Nicodemus, Jesus used the term "born again" to describe the regeneration of the heart accomplished by the Holy Spirit. (John 3:1-21)

[110] Watson, *Repentance*, 102.

12:33) He even warned that his disciples will be persecuted.[111] When faced with the challenge to give up worldly comforts and pleasures, we are tempted to avoid complete surrender to Christ as Lord. "The world so engrosses men's time and bewitches their affections that they cannot repent."[112]

The central issue of this matter is in what we love most. If we love the world and its sinful lusts more than anything else, then we would certainly be miserable without them. But if we love God supremely, then he alone is what we crave most.[113] No other delight can compare with our enjoyment of him. Genuine repentance, then, is a change in attitude about God. To love him is our highest calling. To obey him is our deepest desire. To know him as father is our greatest honor.

> For this is the love of God, that we keep his commandments. And his commandments are not burdensome. For everyone who has been born of God overcomes the world. And this is the victory that has overcome the world--our faith. (1 John 5:3-4)

Shame. Another unpleasant consequence which may prevent some from coming to Christ is that his gospel is considered foolish to the world. "For the word of the cross is folly to those who are perishing, but to us who are being saved it is the power of God." (1 Corinthians 1:18) However, Jesus offers a strong deterrent to the fear of man. He said "do not fear those who kill the body but cannot kill the soul. Rather fear him who can destroy both soul and body in hell." (Matthew 10:28) Watson restates this verse poignantly by saying, "It is better that men should reproach you for repenting than that God should damn you for not repenting."[114]

---

[111] See Mathew 5:10-11. See also 2 Timothy 3:12 in which Paul warns that Christians should expect persecution.

[112] Watson, *Repentance*, 105.

[113] As an example Psalm 42:1 reads, "As a deer pants for flowing streams, so pants my soul for you, O God."

[114] Watson, *Repentance*, 105.

The Means to Repentance

In the Old Testament, obedience to God's Law was of primary importance. Rituals were practiced at certain intervals and in prescribed ways, in order to symbolically cleanse God's people from their sins. Sacrifices, for example, had to be repeated over and over because no one could consistently keep the whole Law. At the dawning of the New Testament, though, this outward Law was fulfilled by God himself through changing the hearts of His people. He "put his holy law into our inward nature."[115]

When the Law is written on a man's heart, he is no longer content with worshiping himself. Rather, he is fully devoted to a new master – Jesus Christ. And, as Jesus came to "fulfill the Law" (Matt. 5:17), so the Christ-follower delights in obeying it. Thus, to the regenerate heart in a repentant sinner "holiness becomes a pleasure, and sin becomes a sorrow."[116] The Law, then, shows us our *need* of repentance and helps us to see that we *have* repented.

Within this framework, there are some very specific truths regarding how repentance occurs. First, it is brought about by the Word of God. In Peter's sermon at Pentecost we read that "when they heard [that the man they crucified actually was the Messiah] they were cut to the heart, and said... what shall we do?" (Acts 2:37) Peter's response was that they should "repent and be baptized... for the forgiveness of sins." (Acts 2:38) Second, as we've already recognized, the Holy Spirit regenerates the heart so that a person desires to repent. And third, we must appreciate that repentance is a gift from God. We see this in Acts 11:18, which says "God has granted to the Gentiles also the repentance that leads to life."

But what if you have seen your need to repent, yet you do not see any *fruit* of repentance in your life? How do you proceed to actually repent? Repentance is both sought and expressed in prayer. A good example is the prayer of David recorded in Psalm 51, which he composed after being confronted regarding his sin of adultery with Bathsheba, and the subsequent murder of her husband.

---

115 Spurgeon, *Law*, 26.

116 Ibid, 29.

To the choirmaster. A Psalm of David, when Nathan the prophet went to him, after he had gone in to Bathsheba.

1 Have mercy on me, O God, according to your steadfast love; according to your abundant mercy blot out my transgressions.

2 Wash me thoroughly from my iniquity, and cleanse me from my sin!

3 For I know my transgressions, and my sin is ever before me.

4 Against you, you only, have I sinned and done what is evil in your sight, so that you may be justified in your words and blameless in your judgment.

5 Behold, I was brought forth in iniquity, and in sin did my mother conceive me.

6 Behold, you delight in truth in the inward being, and you teach me wisdom in the secret heart.

7 Purge me with hyssop, and I shall be clean; wash me, and I shall be whiter than snow.

8 Let me hear joy and gladness; let the bones that you have broken rejoice.

9 Hide your face from my sins, and blot out all my iniquities.

10 Create in me a clean heart, O God, and renew a right spirit within me.

11 Cast me not away from your presence, and take not your Holy Spirit from me.

12 Restore to me the joy of your salvation, and uphold me with a willing spirit.

13 Then I will teach transgressors your ways, and sinners will return to you.

14 Deliver me from bloodguiltiness, O God, O God of my salvation, and my tongue will sing aloud of your righteousness.

15 O Lord, open my lips, and my mouth will declare your praise.

> [16] For you will not delight in sacrifice, or I would give it; you will not be pleased with a burnt offering.
> [17] The sacrifices of God are a broken spirit; a broken and contrite heart, O God, you will not despise.
> [18] Do good to Zion in your good pleasure; build up the walls of Jerusalem;
> [19] then will you delight in right sacrifices, in burnt offerings and whole burnt offerings; then bulls will be offered on your altar.

Notice the way this poem is structured, that each confession of sin in the beginning correlates precisely to its sanctified counterpart toward the end of the psalm.[117] Once the climactic point of repentance has been reached in his plea for restoration (verse 8), the following relationships become evident:

> A broken covenant (paraphrased from title) becomes a restored relationship (19).
> His plea for self-restoration (1-2) becomes a plea for national restoration (18).
> A recognition of sin (3-4) becomes confidence to live in holiness (13-15, 16-17).
> He confesses a wicked heart (5) and asks that it be transformed (11-12).
> He declares that God changes hearts (6) and asks for a new one (10).
> He begs for cleansing (7) and thereby prays for forgiveness (9).

This psalm serves as an example of a repenting heart that seeks to be transformed from the inside out. Counselor and author David Covington suggests that "our prayers of repentance must bring us, as [King] David's

---

[117] See David Covington, "Psalm 51: Repenter's Guide." *JBC* 20 (2001): 25 for a full description of the chiastic structure in this psalm. See also 2 Samuel 11 for the entire account of King David's sin with Bathsheba.

brought him, to the cross."[118] The utter depravity of our wicked hearts must be put to death with Christ by repentance. Only then can we be given new birth, just as Christ himself was raised from the dead. Only through repentance can we be saved from eternal condemnation and enabled to "walk in newness of life." (Rom. 6:4)

Notice also that the only *actions* mentioned in the psalm are those which stem from King David's regenerate heart. He does not propose to do good deeds without godly sorrow, and then demand forgiveness based on those actions. Nor does he blame external circumstances. He could have blamed Bathsheba for bathing in sight of him. Or, he could have blamed God for making *her* so beautiful and giving *him* sexual desire. Instead of blameshifting, though, King David "knew that his guilt began with the condition of his heart."[119] We can learn from this psalm how to use prayer in exposing the sinfulness of our hearts, acquiring a godly sorrow for personal wickedness, and seeking reconciliation to God through repentance.

Conclusion

A true Christian has a continual sense of his own degradation, and a deep sorrow for exposed sin. He does not detest the Law, or wish to change it. Rather, he receives it and desires to obey it. He sees that the Law is right in condemning him, but his repentant heart celebrates the work of Christ in saving him. This is possible because God has replaced his "heart of stone" with a "heart of flesh." (Ezekiel 36:26) And the result is that a sinner saved by grace has been made "alive together with Christ," so consider yourselves dead to sin and alive to God in Christ Jesus." (Ephesians 2:5, Romans 6:11)

The greatest test of genuine repentance, then, lays "not so much in what you *do* as what you *delight to do*."[120] When one dies to self, he lives to

[118] Covington, *Psalm 51*, 34.

[119] Ibid, 28.

[120] Spurgeon, *Law*, 29.

Christ. This transaction, stemming from God's regeneration of a person's heart, is the way in which Christ's atoning sacrifice is made applicable to us. We die with him. We live with Him. Thus, genuine repentance is *dying in order to live.*[121]

[121] See Appendix A for more on the application of repentance, through the exegesis of Colossians 3:1-11. It is too technical for inclusion here, and is not essential to answering the question at hand, but is beneficial for further study.

Question 3

Do I Have to Believe in the Resurrection of Christ?

Introduction

It has been said that "Christianity is an Easter faith."[122] This is because the resurrection of Christ has been a prominent belief and teaching throughout the history of the church.[123] For Christians, our hope in life both now and in the future is rooted in the idea of living *in* Christ. In essence, "the Last Day at the end of history had taken shape on the third day in the midst of history."[124] Moreover, if Jesus was the prophesied Messiah then the "last days" had surely begun.[125] The church has therefore historically recognized the risen and exalted Jesus as its head. So, when Jesus gave Peter a mandate

[122] Michael Ramsey, *The Resurrection of Christ: An Essay in Biblical Theology* (London, England: Lowe and Brydone, 1956), 90.

[123] Ibid, 102. The Christian conviction regarding the afterlife is grounded in Jesus' promise that we will be with Him.

[124] Neville Clark, *Interpreting the Resurrection* (London, England: SCM Press, 1967), 52.

[125] Ibid, 59. See also 1 Peter 1:5.

to proclaim the resurrection, the church did so and has continued to do so ever since.[126]

If the resurrection is so important to the church, then perhaps it is crucial in the acquiring of salvation for each individual. Most of the time the *death* of Christ is our focus with regard to salvation, because only through his paying the penalty for our sins can we be pardoned on judgment day. However, must one also believe in Jesus' *resurrection* in order to be saved? To answer this question, following is a summary of the main positions and an argument that belief in Jesus' death and resurrection cannot be separated in the mind of a true Christian.

Survey of Positions

It should first be stated that there were no claims of resurrection prior to the biblical account, not even of great martyrs. Thus, the resurrection debates of early Christian history occurred because "something extraordinary had clearly happened."[127] We will therefore begin with the assumption that Jesus' resurrection is a valid historical event, and thereby simply focus on the necessity of belief in this event as it relates to the Christian view of salvation.

Position 1 – Belief is Necessary for Salvation

Corporate doctrine. The early church proclaimed that confession of Jesus as Lord was the means by which a person could escape God's wrath and instead receive eternal life. In order for Jesus to be Lord, however, He must be alive in either physical body or in spirit. Hence, belief in the resurrection was tied directly to belief in the crucifixion, since one aspect of faith could not exist without the other.[128] This is because the Christian

[126] Miles Coverdale, "The Resurrection of Christ," in *Writings and Translations of Miles Coverdale, Bishop of Exeter*, ed. George Pearson (Cambridge, England: The University Press, 1844), 325.

[127] Alister McGrath, *Resurrection* (Minneapolis, MN: Fortress Press, 2008), 29.

[128] George Elden Ladd, *I Believe in the Resurrection of Jesus* (Grand Rapids, MI: William B. Eerdman's Publishing, 1975), 146. Ladd states that "if Jesus is dead the

agrees that the historic event of resurrection happened, while at the same time trusting in Jesus' death as payment for sins. Thus, forgiveness of sins is found in the same man who was both crucified and raised. The Apostle Paul stated early Christian doctrine most clearly as follows:

> 9 If you confess with your mouth Jesus *as* Lord, and believe in your heart that God raised Him from the dead, you will be saved." (Romans 10:9)[129]

There are many New Testament assertions that "Jesus is Lord," in many of which the verb is present tense because these Christians actually believed Jesus had been raised and exalted by God.[130] Still today necessity of resurrection is seen from two aspects. First, that Jesus did rise from the dead. And second, that because He lives He is able to return physically to the earth again. Thus, the majority opinion is an *already-not yet* tension that has been held for centuries without confusion or debate.[131]

Personal doctrine. Faith in God, plus a *person's* sacrifice, was necessary to please God in the Old Covenant. But in the New Covenant faith in God plus faith in *His* sacrifice is the precondition for salvation.[132] This is why the inspired writings of the New Testament canon assert repeatedly that believing in the resurrection of Christ is a significant part of the faith required of each person.[133] We must have faith not only in the death of Christ, but also in His life thereafter.

Consider, for example, that I ask my wife to provide tea with our family meal. She would not simply put tea bags on the table beside my

---

heart of New Testament Christology is also a delusion."

[129] Unless otherwise specified, all Scripture quotations in this chapter are taken from the NASB translation. See also Acts 2:36.

[130] Ramsey, *Resurrection of Christ*, 90.

[131] Richard B. Gaffin, Jr. "Redemption and Resurrection: An Exercise in Biblical-Systematic Theology," in *A Confessing Theology for Postmodern Times*, ed. Michael S. Horton (Wheaton, IL:Crossway Books, 2000), 234. See also 2 Cor. 4:16 for Paul's contrast between the outer man and the inner man, one being presently realized and the other to be realized in the future.

[132] Paul Bourgy, *The Resurrection of Christ and of Christians* (Dubuque, IA:The Priory Press, 1963), 48.

[133] See Rom. 10:9 and 1 Thes. 4:14.

plate. Rather, she understands that tea is more than just leaves of a plant. The tea that I requested also includes water and, being from the southern U.S., lots of sugar. Similarly, our faith is in the entire person of Jesus Christ, so that any historical event in which he is involved becomes part of our faith as well. Hence, "our salvation is necessarily bound to the risen Christ."[134]

A new covenant. Throughout redemptive history God has been active in drawing to himself a people to call his own. In the opening pages of our New Testament, we even see the gospel writer using harvest language to describe God's ingathering of His elect.[135] And in the Easter story "the resurrection-harvest at the end of history is already visible."[136]

In the New Covenant, physical birth into the Israelite community is no longer the mark of spiritual privilege. Likewise, the old order of religious rituals has also been dissolved so that anyone can become a son of God through a new order which is directly tied to the resurrection.[137] "For if we have been united with him in a death like his, we shall certainly be united with him in a resurrection like his."[138]

Validation of messiahship. The most commonly asserted notion regarding the significance of resurrection is the idea that it proved Jesus' identity as not only a man, but also as God in the flesh. In His traceable human lineage, the crucifixion and resurrection confirmed His legal descent through the line of David. According to Old Testament prophecy, He could therefore truly be the Messiah.[139] Christians believe that it

---

[134] Bourgy, *Resurrection of Christ*, 48-49.

[135] See Matt. 3:7-12 for the narrative of John the Baptist proclaiming a harvest soon to come.

[136] Gaffin, *Redemption and Resurrection*, 233.

[137] McGrath, *Resurrection*, 55.

[138] See Rom. 6:5 (ESV).

[139] McGrath, *Resurrection*, 54. See also Jer. 30:9 which says that God's people "shall serve the LORD their God and David their king, whom [God] will raise up for them." This heir of David who would be raised up to kingly status is also prophesied by King David himself to be God's Holy One who would not "see corruption." This is evident in Psalm 16:10, which Peter quotes in his great sermon in Acts 2:25-31, saying specifically that "[David] foresaw and spoke about the resurrection of Christ."

was "Jesus' own resurrection which constituted him as Messiah, and, if Messiah, then Lord of the world."[140]

Of further importance is the New Testament narration that with Jesus came the inauguration of His Kingdom.[141] The resurrection validated His claim to be King, so that His message of the Kingdom's arrival could also be believed.[142] Hence, the church's foundational identity – that it is the visible, present aspect of His Kingdom – could rightly be upheld due to a literal, historical, bodily resurrection.[143]

Position 2 – Belief is Not Necessary for Salvation

Belief is not mandated. Outside of Paul's writings, there is no biblical support for insisting upon belief in the resurrection as a requirement for salvation. In fact, in the resurrection narratives "at no point does Jesus or anyone else mention the future hope for believers [resurrection vicariously through Christ] – neither in terms of the hope of heaven or salvation."[144] Because the Bible is authoritative for the orthodox Christian, one cannot presume the necessity of belief in resurrection if the Bible does not clearly teach it.

Belief is difficult. Furthermore, it is difficult for modern Christians to believe every aspect of the biblical accounts. And the more difficult it is to believe, the more one questions its necessity as important doctrine. Miles Coverdale, former bishop of Exeter in the 1500's, offers a helpful observation for considering the insignificance of the resurrection with regard to salvation. He suggested that the story of "doubting" Thomas reassures those of us who doubt the resurrection. His intent was that this

---

140 N.T. Wright, "Jesus' Resurrection and Christian Origins," in *Passionate Conviction: Contemporary Discourses on Christian Apologetics,* ed. Paul Copan, William Lane Craig (Nashville, TN: B & H Publishing Group, 2007), 129. See also *Resurrection,* DVD, dir. N. T. Wright (Downer's Grove, IL: IVP Connect, 2009).

141 See Matt. 4:17, Mark 1:15, and Luke 8:1.

142 See Matt. 27:11, Mark 15:2, and Luke 23:3 for Jesus' assertion that He is King of the Jews. See also John 2:19 for Jesus' promise to rebuild a new temple, His church, in three days.

143 Clark, *Interpreting the Resurrection*, 46 and 54.

144 McGrath, *Resurrection*, 38.

reference would cause us to see the importance in believing. For this story to be included in John's account, Coverdale asserted, it must be important to establish that Jesus' physical body was literally raised to live again.[145] An antagonist, however, could argue that the story is there to demonstrate that even a person who has to "see it to believe it" can still be a true disciple. In fact, there are many other accounts of the disciples not expecting, nor initially believing in, Jesus' resurrection.[146] Even Jesus' disciples, with whom He was physically present during His earthly ministry, did not easily recognize Him. Although He had told them numerous times that He would be raised, they were surprised when it happened.[147] If it was difficult for them to believe, how could we be required to believe over two thousand years later?

In the early 20th Century, Friedrich Schleiermacher rejected the notion that miracles actually happened, including the miraculous resurrection of Jesus. He asserted that for us to believe in the resurrection is a psychological notion with no necessary root in historical fact. For him, the resurrection becomes what we make of it, which means that we cannot be held responsible for belief in it.[148] Furthermore, he suggests that if Jesus does have immortality it is the same immortality as the rest of humanity.[149]

Other Christian theologians have argued that the resurrection was only symbolic, or that it only involved Jesus' spiritual dimension.[150] In either case, they detract from any urgency in believing a literal and bodily resurrection of the Christ.

Considering just these few viewpoints, we can see enough digression from orthodoxy to assess typical patterns of unbelief. The struggle seems to be with one underlying question. If we can't believe it, then how can we be judged by it?

---

145 Coverdale, *Resurrection of Christ*, 345.

146 See Luke 24:11, 24:16, 24:37.

147 See Matt. 16:21, 17:23, 20:19.

148 Douglass Farrow, "Resurrection and Immortality," in *The Oxford Handbook of Systematic Theology*, ed. John Webster, Kathryn Tanner, Iain Torrance (New York, NY: Oxford University Press, 2007), 224.

149 Ibid, 231.

150 Farrow, *Resurrection and Immortality*, 225.

Support for My Position

Atonement Necessitates Victory

The cross is not just a morally influential event, provoking us to live in appreciation of Jesus' suffering. Nor is the cross an example of righteous suffering that we should follow. Rather, the cross was "real atonement – a substitutionary, expiatory sacrifice that reconciles God to sinners and propitiates his judicial wrath."[151]

Historically, both Catholic and Protestant Christians have given most of their attention to the death of Christ, rather than His resurrection. This is largely due to the necessity of repentance in the conversion of a sinner. The church has rightly emphasized that, "as with her Lord, the way to resurrection lies through the road of death."[152] Every believer must die vicariously with Christ in order to become unified with Him in resurrection. Fortunately for us, the way of death for God's children is through repentance rather than a literal, physical death. And once the old nature is considered dead, the new Christian has the assurance of living eternally under the gracious control of Jesus Christ. Hence, repentance is dying in order that we may live.[153]

It must be emphasized that salvation accomplished by Christ is more than just atonement through his death. The resurrection event after the cross is also a necessary aspect of Christian faith. Because Christ was raised we know that He truly was the predicted Messiah. As Messiah, then, we are affirmed in believing that His suffering and death were for *us*. Therefore, "the cross and resurrection stood forth together as the blazing heart of God's final deed of redemption."[154] Together, His death and new life work

---

[151] Gaffin, *Redemption and Resurrection*, 231. See also Russell Moore, "Models of the Atonement" (classroom lecture, 27070 – *Systematic Theology, Pt. 2*, 5 November 2009). Moore labels the models referenced here as Moral Influence and Moral Example. Note that the term *expiatory* means here the ability to make atonement. And the meaning of *propitiate* is to appease.

[152] Clark, *Interpreting the Resurrection*, 61. See also Col. 3:3.

[153] See chapter two for a more detailed treatment of this concept that repentance is *dying in order to live.*

[154] Clark, *Interpreting the Resurrection*, 52.

to atone for sin – one act validating the other. In the resurrection God exalted His Son and thus claimed victory over death forever.[155] Scripture therefore pronounces that Jesus' victory over death is shared with those who believe.[156]

> **8** Now if we have died with Christ, we believe that we shall also live with Him, **9** knowing that Christ, having been raised from the dead, is never to die again; death no longer is master over Him. **10** For the death that He died, He died to sin once for all; but the life that He lives, He lives to God. **11** Even so consider yourselves to be dead to sin, but alive to God in Christ Jesus. (Romans 6:8-11)

A New Man

We should be careful, though, not to simply define resurrection as a symbol of the real meaning behind the cross. Rather, "it is the *new deed* of God which makes Calvary significant."[157] Immediately after the resurrection, and certainly because of the resurrection, Jesus "breathed on [the disciples]" much like God breathed life into Adam.[158] This was an "act of new creation."[159] This sequence of events was the dawn of a new creation, a new genealogy for mankind.[160]

Our faith is emboldened by the resurrection because just as Jesus took on flesh and now lives forever, so too can the rest of us who have been

---

[155] Ibid, 55.

[156] Ibid, 57. Clark says that "to overwhelm sin is to rob death of its sting." See also George A. Maloney, *The First Day of Eternity: Resurrection Now* (London, England: Sheed and Ward, 1982), 56.

[157] See Clark, *Interpreting the Resurrection*, 100, who reminds us that the apostles' testimonies emphasized that this was a new deed of God. See also Gaffin, *Redemption and Resurrection*, 231, who reiterates that the resurrection does not just prove Christ's deity.

[158] See John 20:22 and Gen. 2:7.

[159] Ramsey, *Resurrection of Christ*, 87.

[160] See 2 Cor. 5:17 and Gal. 6:15.

born of the flesh. The flesh, in this sense, is a "vehicle for the glory of God."[161] As such, in the future our bodies will be like Jesus' resurrected body.[162] Therefore, Jesus was the "first fruits" of a new creation.[163] The biblical imagery of first fruits necessarily implies that there is more fruit to come. Otherwise, it wouldn't be first of anything thereafter and could not accurately be labeled *first*. Hence, "the resurrection of Christ and of believers cannot be separated."[164] If He is the first fruit, as the Bible clearly asserts, then His resurrection is necessary in order for Christians to have hope in their own future resurrection.[165]

In order for Christ to be the first fruit of a new breed of men, He had to have been fully human during His lifetime and then also raised to a fully human existence in the same way that *we* will be. Therefore, "the resurrection… is not so much an especially evident display or powerful proof of Christ's *divine* nature as it is the powerful transformation of his *human* nature."[166]

Being first fruit also means that Christ personally received what He previously did not have, which was a spiritual body. This is to say that at the resurrection the Spirit empowered Jesus as was not so before.[167] Thus, through the resurrection and ascension Jesus took on a glorified human nature in which the Holy Spirit indwells the human body. In actuality, then, our hope for a genuinely new life is that "the resurrection constitutes Him in the image to which believers are predestined to be conformed – we are being transformed into his resurrected likeness, not his crucified likeness."[168] If we were only to be like Him in His death, we would not have the assurance of eternal life through the indwelling presence of the

---

161 Veselin Kesich, *The First Day of the New Creation: The Resurrection and the Christian Faith* (Crestwood, NY: St. Vladimir's Seminary Press, 1982), 135-136.

162 Ibid, 147. See also Phil. 3:21 and 1 Cor. 15:44.

163 See 1 Cor. 15:20, 23.

164 Gaffin, *Redemption and Resurrection*, 232.

165 See also Rom. 8:23, James 1:18, and Rev. 14:4 for additional uses of the term *first fruits* in relation to Christians.

166 Gaffin, *Redemption and Resurrection*, 233. See also 1 Cor. 6:13-15, which describes how our bodies and Jesus' body are united through resurrection.

167 See Rom. 1:4 and 2 Cor. 13:4.

168 Gaffin, *Redemption and Resurrection*, 236. See also Rom. 8:29-30.

Holy Spirit.[169] But since Jesus was raised and enjoined with the Spirit, in Him we may share the same kind of existence forever.

It should further be pointed out that, from a human perspective, Jesus was raised by the Father. Scripture emphasizes "the creative power and action of the Father, of which Christ is the recipient."[170] Just as God created man, so too is God responsible for re-creating man through the resurrection of Jesus Christ.[171] It should be noted, however, that this is not to contradict Jesus' own claim that he was able to raise himself. In the sense that Jesus is part of the trinity, being fully God and fully man simultaneously, Jesus certainly has power and authority to do all things. However, in the sense that Jesus was the perfect human being who died in the place of all others, he is also described as having been raised by the father.[172]

Resurrection language in the New Testament often employs past tense verbs which indicate something completed within believers.[173] Thus, resurrection life is a realized experience in the life of a believer.[174] It is on this premise that we are to demonstrate a reversal in conduct from walking in deadness of sin to walking "in good works of new-creation existence in Christ."[175] "Dying to their own self-centeredness, the Christians enter a new life wherein the center is not themselves but the risen Christ."[176] So, the resurrection involves "the hope of transformation in the face of personal weakness, failure, sin and despair."[177]

---

169 See 2 Cor. 1:22.

170 Gaffin, *Redemption and Resurrection*, 233. See also Clark, *Interpreting the Resurrection*, 98, who says "the empty tomb stands as the massive sign that the eschatological deed of God is not outside this world of time and space or in despair of it, but has laid hold on it, penetrated deep into it, shattered it, and begun its transformation." See also Gal. 1:1.

171 See 2 Cor. 5:17, which states that "if anyone is in Christ, he is a *new creature*; the old things passed away; behold, *new things* have come.")

172 See John 2:19 and 10:18 for Jesus' claim to have resurrection power. See also Acts 3:15 which states that "God raised him from the dead."

173 See Eph. 2:5-6, Col. 2:12-13, 3:1.

174 See Eph. 2:1, 5.

175 Gaffin, *Redemption and Resurrection*, 234. See also Eph. 2:10.

176 Ramsey, *Resurrection of Christ*, 93.

177 McGrath, *Resurrection*, 57. See also Col. 2:9-12 which describes "the removal of the body of the flesh." See also Clark, *Interpreting the Resurrection*, 62, who reminds

A New Nation

Through death and resurrection, Jesus became the head of the new Israel. In like manner, the new Israelites – Christians – are those who identify with Christ by faith in His death and resurrection. This is why forgiveness is biblically connected with one's baptism, which is a symbolic demonstration of one's internal death through repentance and faith.[178] Moreover, as a person comes up out of the baptismal waters we see a symbol of his or her resurrection to new life in Christ. The life of the baptizing church, then, also correlates to the resurrected life of Christ. And if His physical body is alive in heaven, then also alive is His new earthly body which is the church. This is why it can be said that during this present age "it is through the church that [Jesus] lives and works."[179] In other words, His physical presence on earth is now in a body called the church which is made up of newborn, baptized children of God.

Jesus was not just the first to be raised chronologically, but the first part of a whole that would eventually be presented. His being raised signifies the resurrection of others with Him, in order that He would remain head of the community given Him as an inheritance from the Father.[180] This inheritance is only rightly given to the genuine firstborn. And because Jesus was the firstborn who would never die, only He could claim the eternal inheritance of the saints. Whereas Adam was the firstborn of wickedness, Christ is the firstborn of a new holy lineage.[181] This is important to modern day Christians because He is the "firstborn among *many*."[182] If we desire

---

us of Paul's description in Gal. 3:27 that Christians "have clothed yourselves with Christ." Furthermore, Rom. 6:12-13 asserts newness of the believer's life by exhorting them to "present yourselves to God as those alive from the dead, and your members as instruments of righteousness to God." According to 1 John 3:14, even love for fellow believers is possible only because "we have passed out of death into life" through resurrection.

178 Ramsey, *Resurrection of Christ*, 89-90.

179 Ibid, 94. See also 1 Cor. 12:12.

180 Clark, *Interpreting the Resurrection*, 59. See also 1 Cor. 15:20.

181 Ibid, 59. See also Col. 1:18, in which Jesus' headship is in view. In 1 Cor. 15:22 we see that in Adam all die, but through Jesus all may live. Also, Rev. 1:5 describes Jesus as the firstborn who will receive the inheritance.

182 See Rom. 8:29.

to be counted among His inheritance, then, we must be united to the one for whom the inheritance was purchased.[183]

Absolute Truth

Although the Bible is quite clear that the resurrection is significant with regard to a new race of mankind, and therefore a new holy nation has been established, the most urgent reason that a true Christian must believe in Jesus' resurrection is indicative in their biblical name. While the term *Christian* is common today, the Bible often uses the term *believer,* and for very good reason. Because saving faith always involves belief in something, it is in one sense pointless to debate over whether or not events are *worthy* of believing. The Israelites themselves were condemned because they refused to believe. This is evident in the historical event of the crucifixion, which was "Israel's rejection of God's sovereign word and work in Jesus."[184]

If we were to understand fully the significance of Jesus' death and resurrection, our faith would indeed be perfect. To strengthen our imperfect faith, then, the resurrection should be proclaimed steadily. After all, if one can believe in a dead man being raised then he can believe everything else that has to do with that risen man.[185] The key factor in whether or not one believes is rooted in one's viewpoint with regard to truth. If a person believes that God has given absolute truth within Scripture, then that person can trust it to convey the information necessary for saving faith. As such, "rejecting God's revelation of a risen Christ in the gospel narratives is to rebel against the truth of God himself."[186]

---

[183] See 1 Cor. 15:42-49, which describes that although Adam was head of the first age, Jesus is head of the new age. See also Eph. 2:4-7, which says that God "made us alive together with Christ" and "raised us up with Him," in order to demonstrate His glory "in the ages to come."

[184] Clark, *Interpreting the Resurrection*, 48. See also Psalm 118:22, which describes Jesus as "the stone which the builders rejected" but "has become the chief corner stone."

[185] Coverdale, *Resurrection of Christ*, 323.

[186] Karl Barth, *The Resurrection of the Dead* (New York, NY: Fleming H. Revell Company, 1933), 157. See also 1 Cor. 15:15, which says that in doubting the resurrection "we testified against God that He raised Christ."

"Christian faith has meaning insofar as it is established and grounded in God's saving activity."[187] A denial of Jesus' resurrection would therefore be a rejection of either God's revelation of saving activity in the Bible, or of God's saving activity itself. However, both God's words and actions must be believed together or else there is no faith at all. A denial of the resurrection, then, is a denial of God's words in the Bible, which is rebellion against the truth of God himself. In other words, to be a Christian one must believe in the resurrection because in the Bible God has revealed it to be true. Otherwise, we have no faith in God at all and certainly, then, no hope of salvation.

Objections to My Position

Living in the Land of Make-Believe

The first argument against my position is rooted in the idolatrous act of self-worship first evidenced in the Garden of Eden. Just as Eve was tempted, so too all living beings desire to continue living forever. We humans, therefore, have always sought for ways to preserve our existence. When all our attempts have proven futile, we have then sought to be relieved of our conscious hopelessness by conceiving a believable and rewarding destination after the present life has ended. A particularly satisfying belief for Christians is bodily resurrection from death into a better world. However, we also desire tangible proof that demonstrates the validity of our theory of the afterlife so that we may confidently hope in it. For us, the desired proof of life after death is seen in the supposed resurrection of one man in history, Jesus Christ.[188]

Some would argue that Christians, desiring to hope in life after death, contrived mythical stories to validate their assertions. In order to break the cycle of death, a new generation of man was needed. Therefore, a perfect

[187] David L. Mueller, *Foundation of Karl Barth's doctrine of Reconciliation: Jesus Christ Crucified and Risen*. (New York, NY: Edwen Mellen Press, 1990), 98.
[188] Ludwig Feuerbach, *The Essence of Christianity* (New York, NY: Harper and Brothers, 1957), 135.

man who died and then arose would signify the beginning of a new, immortal kind of person. However, in order for that man to be perfect he had to be miraculously conceived, which meant that his parents could not be merely human. In Christian history, Catholics have resolved this by making Jesus' mother a holy woman, whereas Protestants have insisted that Jesus only inherited his physical humanness from Mary and his sinless perfection was inherited by the Holy Spirit in a miraculous conception.[189]

The essence of this first objection, then, is that Christians have chosen to believe the lie that Jesus arose, which then necessitated the generation of other lies to cover up the first one. According to this view biblical Christianity is all a hoax, elaborately constructed to prove what one wants to believe.

Invalidating the Atonement

Another significant argument is that, according to our own logic, the atonement would be nullified by Jesus' resurrection. According to this view the death of Christ should be all that is necessary to atone for the sins of humanity, and the resurrection is therefore counterproductive. Jesus' body could have even been cremated with no negative consequence.[190] To exhume the body that was given as a sacrifice for sins actually would reverse the propitiation said to be accomplished through its death. Thus, raising Jesus would invalidate the very means by which He is said to have saved mankind from its depravity. The end result is that the act of resurrection itself would prevent the re-creation of a new man and a new nation.

---

[189] Feuerbach, *Essence of Christianity*, 138.

[190] Theodore M. Drange, "Why Resurrect Jesus?" in *The Empty Tomb,* ed. Robert M. Price, Jeffery Jay Lowder (Amherst, NY: Prometheus Books, 2005), 57. See also Theodore M. Drange, *Nonbelief and Evil* (Amherst, NY: Prometheus Books, 1998) for an exhaustive look at Drange's atheistic perspectives. See also Stephen T. Davis, *Disputed Issues: Contending for Christian Faith in Today's Academic Setting* (Waco, TX: Baylor University Press, 2009) for counterarguments against Drange and others.

Dissimilarity Disproves Unity

A final argument worthy of consideration is the concept that Jesus' resurrection would have been more like ours if He had stayed dead until the second coming.[191] This is a good point because wherever Jesus was, and whatever He was doing for three days prior to Easter Sunday, could have remained His abode until His return at the end of the age. Of further significance is the fact that Jesus' body was not destroyed in the grave as ours will be. This further makes our resurrection different than His.[192] We Christians speak directly from Scripture that Jesus "had to be made *like His brethren in all things*, so that He might become a merciful and faithful high priest in things pertaining to God, to make propitiation for the sins of the people."[193] By asserting that Jesus has to be just like us in order to redeem us, but that His resurrection is not like ours, our argument is seen to contradict itself and become incredible. Once again, Jesus could not initiate a new man and a new nation because, according to our own reasoning, He cannot be both the same and different simultaneously.

Defense of My Position

Dissimilarity Overcome by Spiritual Unity

Unbelief regarding the resurrection has been considered heretical since the earliest years of the church. And, the deadening (pun intended) of resurrection significance is still common in many churches today. For example, we may hear someone say at a funeral something like, "That is just Joe's shell lying there, but we know he is really with Jesus." Such preaching minimizes the importance of the resurrection to genuine Christian faith by separating the physical realm from the spiritual.

Seeking to spiritualize tangible events such as the resurrection, a person may argue from 1 Cor. 15:50 that because "flesh and blood cannot inherit

---

[191] Drange, *Empty Tomb*, 61.

[192] Drange, *Empty Tomb*, 62.

[193] Heb. 2:17

the kingdom" our physical bodies will not literally be raised. It may be suggested that our inner spiritual body is all that may continue forever, and a continuation of spiritual life does not necessitate bodily resurrection.[194]

This view, that we need to be saved spiritually rather than physically, describes "no more than resuscitation, and not true Christian resurrection."[195] It "overturns God's entire plan for man's salvation, which is the resurrection of the body."[196] As Irenaeus argued, "if the resurrection is only spiritual, then the created world... is not saved."[197] Instead, we should recognize that in 1 Cor. 15 Paul was describing the *works* of the flesh and not the *body* itself. The first fourteen chapters of Paul's letter to the Corinthians demonstrates that he knew well what it meant for man to live in this present world. And, he does not teach the idea that our physical existence is unrelated to our core reality as an immortal spirit.[198] What Paul means is that "man as flesh cannot enter the kingdom, yet flesh, the material substance, the body in itself, can be transformed and brought under the rule and power of the Spirit. Flesh is capable of corruption, but also of incorruption."[199]

The Christian life, and thus also the life of the church, is resurrection-life given through the Holy Spirit.[200] But we do not seek only spiritual life because to do so would imply "the prolongation of man's finite existence for everlasting years."[201] On the contrary, believing that our bodies will

[194] See Ramsey, *Resurrection of Christ*, 102, who points out that "Jews believed in the resurrection of the body... But nowhere, either for Greek or for Jew, was belief in the future life vivid, immediate, central and triumphant."

[195] See Maloney, *First Day*, 46-47, who also points out that the philosophy of Platonism as the driving force behind this view.

[196] Kerich, *First Day*, 134.

[197] Ibid, 134.

[198] Rudolf Bultmann, *Faith and Understanding* (New York, NY: Harper and Row, 1966), 82. The term for this philosophical concept is monism. See also Mueller, *Barth's Doctrine*, 101, who argues that though the Corinthians held to monism, "true believers hold to a Christian dualism which acknowledges the tension between promise and fulfillment."

[199] Kesich, *First Day*, 135.

[200] Gaffin, *Redemption and Resurrection*, 239. See also 1 Cor. 15:45

[201] Ramsey, *Resurrection of Christ*, 101.

someday rise again with Christ gives us the comfort of hope.[202] And this hope is impressed upon us by the work of the Holy Spirit after we have been resurrected to new life in Christ through our faith. By faith we seek to be conformed to the image of Christ, an image which must be alive or else we would be longing only for death.[203] As "we have borne the image of the man of dust," so "we shall also bear the image of the man of heaven."[204]

The Spirit is given to bear witness to His victory over death, and to make fully known what is accomplished in His resurrection. Thus, we are given the Spirit just as Jesus was enjoined to the Spirit so that the core spiritual existence of both may live together forever. Though the physical body is not necessary for existence, it is part of the promise that we will be raised *like* Christ – yet not *identically as* Christ.

Atonement Requires Resurrection

"Death is in the world as the pinnacle of all rebellion against God; and death will be overcome some day."[205] Central to the Christian faith is that death has been overcome by our King. Hence, "a dead Messiah cannot be Messiah at all."[206] The Apostle Paul taught that the first Adam granted us death, whereas the second Adam (Jesus) granted us resurrection life. Paul spoke of our atonement as being a free gift of righteousness, a righteousness accomplished by Jesus' action, and a righteousness that results in life through Jesus – presupposing that Jesus is alive or else our righteous standing would cease to be alive. Consider the text of this argument from the book of Romans, as follows:

> 17 For if, because of one man's trespass, death reigned
> through that one man, much more will those who receive
> the abundance of grace and the free gift of righteousness
> reign in life through the one man Jesus Christ. 18 Therefore,

---

202 Coverdale, *Resurrection of Christ*, 323.

203 Kesich, *First Day*, 153.

204 See 1 Cor. 15:49.

205 Bultmann, *Faith and Understanding*, 85.

206 Barth, *Resurrection of Dead*, 156 and 172.

> as one trespass led to condemnation for all men, so one act of righteousness leads to justification and life for all men.
> [19] For as by the one man's disobedience the many were made sinners, so by the one man's obedience the many will be made righteous.[207] (Romans 5:17-19 ESV)

Furthermore, Christ's new kingdom for Paul is seen as a future realization with present implications. This Kingdom is entered into by faith – a hope and expectation of full disclosure. "Faith, i.e, to be in the Kingdom of Christ, means to await resurrection."[208] So, the Kingdom is not simply a continuation of life in another world, but instead is a resurrection from the dead.[209]

> "When Paul speaks of the resurrection of the dead, it is clear that he means to speak of us, of our reality, of our existence, of a reality in which we stand... Our resurrection is, with the resurrection of Christ, a reality."[210]

Truth is Objective

Since perfection is antonymous for our status in this age, we could in no way attain salvation if a perfect comprehension of it were required. Even so, it is unwise for Christians to use generic statements in defense against logical arguments. For example, Charles Hodge once insisted on the necessity of resurrection belief by stating that "all of Christ's claims and the success of His work rest upon the fact that he rose from the dead."[211] Such a defense does more harm than good for the Christian cause since it is so easily refuted.

---

[207] See also 1 Cor. 15:45, which states that "the first man Adam became a living being; the last Adam became a life-giving spirit."

[208] Barth, *Resurrection of Dead*, 172.

[209] Ibid, 172. See also Mueller, *Barth's Doctrine*, 100, for further analysis of Barth's comments.

[210] Bultmann, *Faith and Understanding*, 81.

[211] See Drange, *Empty Tomb*, 59, in which Drange correctly argues against Hodge.

The resurrection is not the only way God could verify the truth of the gospel in Jesus' sonship, divinity, humanity, atonement, or propitiation. Likewise, the resurrection is not the only possible foundation for Jesus to take on the titles of Savior, Messiah, Prophet, Priest, and King.[212] Rather, God could have used a number of other means for verification of who Jesus was and what He accomplished for mankind. For us to assert that God can only accomplish his purposes in one way is to place limitations on a limitless being.

Our belief must rest in God and in His *revealed means* of salvation. Therefore, our best argument is to stand on the authority of Scripture as objective truth directly given by God for the purpose of our salvation through faith. In this way it cannot be said that we are making up stories in order to justify what we want to believe in. Belief in the resurrection, and the salvific necessity of this belief, is ultimately rooted in the foundation that Scripture is true and authoritative.[213]

The biblical witness asserts strongly that resurrection is primarily a "transaction between God and Jesus the Christ, and only then and therefore a transaction between the Christ and the believer."[214] Moreover, God affirmed Jesus' identity in this transaction by raising him from the grave, and believers are raised with Christ through faith.[215] Thus, a true Christian is saved by faith in Jesus' life, death, *and* resurrection.

> [3] Blessed be the God and Father of our Lord Jesus Christ, who according to His great mercy has caused us to be *born again* to a living hope *through the resurrection* of Jesus Christ from the dead, [4] to obtain an inheritance which is imperishable and undefiled and will not fade away, reserved in heaven for you, [5] who are protected by the power of God *through faith* for a salvation ready to be revealed in the last time. (1 Peter 1:3-5)

---

[212] Ibid, 56.

[213] See chapter one for a detailed explanation of how we received the New Testament from God, and why we can trust that the Scriptures we possess are precisely what he intended for us to hold as his written revelation.

[214] Clark, *Interpreting the Resurrection*, 101.

[215] Ibid, 101.

Question 4

Is There an Unforgivable Sin?

Introduction

Near the end of 1 John is a description of intercessory prayer which is often confusing to readers. The passage indicates that there is a type of sin which is unforgiveable, and that we should not even pray for a person guilty of such a sin. This may be alarming to us, since we've come to accept that everyone struggles with sin even after becoming a Christian. However, upon careful consideration we can resolve the peculiarity of this text so that it is useful as both a warning and an encouragement. Therefore, the aim of this chapter will be to propose the most suitable interpretation of the following text:

> 16 If anyone sees his brother committing a sin not leading to death, he shall ask and God will for him give life to those who commit sin not leading to death. There is a sin leading to death; I do not say that he should make request for this. 17 All unrighteousness is sin, and there is a sin not leading to death.[216] (1 John 5:16-17)

---

[216] Unless otherwise specified, all Scripture quotations in this chapter are taken from the NASB translation.

The first step in understanding this passage will be to survey its historical setting and traditional opinions regarding John's intended meaning. Next, the immediately surrounding context, and John's letter as a whole, will shed light on the words and phrases of the focal passage itself. In the end, our goal is to discern the message of hope and promise which John intended to convey to his audience – that the brother who has sinned, but has not rejected the gospel, may receive life through the intercessory prayer of a fellow believer.

Background

When the letter of 1 John was written, about AD 90, the young Christian community was in the process of solidifying foundational tenets for true religion. Jesus, their founder, had long been gone and they had – to our knowledge – no formal compilation of writings to protect his core teaching. New Testament Scriptures were in the process of being written and distributed, but were not yet fully completed. In the absence of scriptural protection, false teachers had arisen both from outside the community and from within. A popular sect, known as Gnostics, denied the true humanity of Jesus and pretended that their γνῶσις (knowledge) was so superior that they could berate others who did not possess it. John intended for his three epistles to expose the error of this false teaching, while also giving needed assurance to confused Christians. He asserted that a sinful man who knows the real Jesus is transformed into a child of God, which results in love toward others rather than hostility in the form of needless debates.

Since this message was quite contrary to much contemporary thinking, John also gives the believer hope in the certainty that this new life in Christ cannot be overcome by the world, and it will never end. A person's hope of eternal life is secured by confidence in God's power, regardless of the believer's weakness against the darkness of the world.[217]

[217] John 20:31 states the author's purpose in writing. He says that "these have been written so that you may believe that Jesus is the Christ, the Son of God; and that believing you may have life in His name."

Contextual Rationale

In the fifth chapter, the author is wrapping up his previous exhortations with a direct application to the believer. Upon close examination, we see that a true Christian can be characterized by the following paraphrased conditional statements:

> If I believe Jesus is Christ, then I am God's child. (5:1a)
> If I love my Father, then I love His other children. (5:1b)
> If I love His other children, then I love and obey my Father. (5:2)
> If I love my Father, then I will obey Him. (5:3)
> If I am His child, then I overcome the world. (5:4a)
> If I have faith, then I overcome the world. (5:4b)
> If I believe Jesus is the Son of God, then I overcome the world. (5:5)
> If I believe Jesus is the Son of God, then God's Spirit revealed it to me. (5:10a)
> If I *do not* believe what God revealed, then I call God a liar. (5:10b)
> If I have the Son of God, then I have eternal life. (5:12a)
> If I *do not* have the Son of God, then I do not have eternal life. (5:12b)

By faith in Christ Jesus, a person is a child of God. As such, he seeks to obey God by loving other believers. He also may have confidence that the world cannot harm him. Hence, the perfect opportunity to see faith grow while also expressing the love of God, is to pray for another who is sinning. In order for the prayer to be answered, though, it must conform to God's will. (5:14) Moreover, the prayer that is certainly God's will is a petition for protection from sin on behalf of another believer. Intercessory prayer, then, is a means by which members of the Christian community strengthen one another. Just as John's purpose in writing is to strengthen believers "who might be tempted to doubt the reality of their Christian experience and to give up their faith in Jesus," he offers prayer as the strengthening action available for every believer to practice against unbelief.[218]

It is important to note that one does not have to be an apostle, an evangelist, a prophet, or a teacher in order to pray. In fact, the apostle Paul teaches that our weakness and ignorance is not a hindrance to prayer because of the overcoming power of the Holy Spirit abiding within us.[219] Although it is clear *who* can pray, *why* we should pray, and *what power* is behind our prayers, it is left unresolved what is the *condition* for which we should *not* pray. Having established the historical context and the rationale behind Paul's teaching in this passage, we can now consider the meaning of the most perplexing phrase.

Traditional Views

In the most debated portion of 1 John 5:16-17, the meaning of what is categorically called a "sin leading to death" has been traditionally viewed in three ways. Following is a brief survey of these common positions.

Categorizing of Sins

This view holds that certain sins are worse than others, based on Old Testament passages which indicate a distinction between intentional and unintentional sins. Whenever a sin is committed by an individual, or the people as a whole, there must be atonement made for it. Sin is never excused without repentance and the offering of a sacrifice as propitiation. The sacrificial offering was acceptable so long as the sin was unintentional, or unknown.[220]

---

[218] I. Howard Marshal, *The Epistles of John,* (Grand Rapids, MI: Eerdmans, 1978), 243.
[219] See Romans 8:26.
[220] Daniel Aikin, *1, 2, and 3 John* (Nashville, TN: Broadman & Holman, 2001), 208. See also Lev. 4:2-3, 13-14, 22, 27; 5:15, 17-18; Num. 15:27-28.

However, if a sin was knowingly committed then the substitutionary sacrifice was not sufficient.[221] The offender himself had to pay the penalty of unrighteousness, which was death.[222] On this basis, during the second century church leaders began to differentiate mortal (deadly) sins from venial (non-deadly) sins. Sins such as murder, adultery, and apostasy could not be forgiven.[223]

The early church found this distinction to be particularly useful in keeping believer's from denying their faith amidst the great persecutions of that era.[224] However, there is insufficient evidence from the New Testament to establish a list of specific sins "leading to death." Furthermore, Paul goes to great lengths explaining that the death of Christ was sufficient for *all* sins committed in the flesh.[225] Thus, the categorization of sins does not sufficiently explain this difficult phrase within our focal passage.

Blasphemy Against the Holy Spirit

Another common view is derived from Matt. 12:32 or Mark 3:28-30, and is even labeled the "unpardonable sin" in many translations. Jesus said that "whoever speaks against the Holy Spirit, it shall not be forgiven him, either in this age or in the age to come."[226] This sin "was a deliberate, open-eyed rejection of known truth," in which a man "willfully sinned against his own conscience."[227] In these examples Jesus' warning was in response to the Pharisees' denial of His source for performing miracles. They insisted

---

[221] Unintentional sins could be classified as "sins of ignorance and sins of weakness." See John Painter, *1, 2, and 3 John*, (Collegeville, MN: Liturgical Press, 2002), 319.
[222] See Aikin, *1, 2, and 3 John*, 208. See also Deut. 17:12-13.
[223] Ibid, 209. Aikin notes that this led to the concept of "seven deadly sins."
[224] Painter, *1, 2, and 3 John*, 318.
[225] See Romans 8:1-4.
[226] See David K. Rensberger, *The Epistles of John*, (Louisville, KY: Westminster John Knox Press, 2001), 96, who disagrees with this parallel. He says that "the language here [1 John 5:16-17] is entirely different from the saying in Mark 3:28-30 about the blasphemy against the Holy Spirit that cannot be forgiven, and there is no reason to connect the two."
[227] John R. W. Stott, *1 John*, in vol. 19 of *The Tyndale New Testament Commentaries*, ed. Leon Morris (Downers Grove, IL: Intervarsity Press, 1988), 191.

that He was empowered by Beelzebub rather than by the Spirit of God. In other words, they failed to "recognize the divine activity in the human life of Jesus."[228] So, what men were rejecting was not the Spirit's power in their own hearts, but rather they doubted the Spirit's involvement in Jesus' miraculous works. They rejected Jesus' divine authority as part of the godhead.

This begs the question, then, as to whether or not man can also reject the Spirit's work within his own heart. There are passages of Scripture which indicate that a man's heart may be hardened so much that he can no longer repent.[229] In these instances it may seem that there are some cases in which a man may reject the Spirit until there is finally no possibility of repentance. However, these passages imply rejection toward God the Father with no mention of God the Spirit. Apparently, we can refuse to see what the Spirit is doing *around* us, but we cannot reject what he is doing *within* us.

Regarding the Spirit's work in saving sinners, we have no textual evidence that the Spirit's effectual calling upon a man's heart is resistible. Rather, we have clear testimony from the Lord himself that a man is reborn by the power of the Spirit, and He says that "all [persons] that the father gives me will come to me."[230] Moreover, the Apostle Paul taught that it is the Spirit who guarantees our inheritance with Christ.[231] Thus, the power of the Spirit in converting sinners, and sustaining their saving faith, is insurmountable by Satan or even by the man himself.[232] In this way Jesus' description of a new, spiritual birth is quite fitting. It is therefore impossible

---

[228] Painter, *1, 2, and 3 John*, 318.

[229] See Hebrews 12:16-17.

[230] See John 6:37. See also John 3:5, "Unless one is born of … the Spirit he cannot enter the kingdom of God."

[231] See Eph. 1:14

[232] See John 6:37-40, Eph. 2:1-10, Col. 1:13, 2:13, John 1:12-13, 3:3, 6:44, Acts 13:48, 16:14, Rom. 8:29-30, and Titus 3:5 for biblical support regarding "irresistible grace" or "effectual calling," meaning the certainty with which the saved are called out by God through the working of the Holy Spirit. See also Eph. 1:13-14, Phil. 1:6, John 10:27-30, and 1 Cor. 6:11 for support regarding the power of the Spirit to protect believers from losing their salvation, a doctrine commonly referred to as the "perseverance of the saints."

for a born-again Christian to reject the Spirit that now lives within him. Although in our Christian walk it is possible, and quite common, to "grieve the Holy Spirit of God" by resisting His influence and continually sinning, we cannot fully reject Him because it is through that same Spirit that we "were sealed for the day of redemption."[233]

Referring to "the sin leading to death" as blasphemy against the spirit is more reasonable than the categorization view, as it does maintain the Romans 8 argument that Jesus' propitiation is for all *fleshly* sins, while also allowing that the "sin leading to death" may be a *spiritual* refusal to claim Christ's propitiation for sin. This rejection of Christ occurs, though, because the Spirit has not regenerated a man's heart. It is unfortunate that this view takes its label from a passage which does not clearly suit the proposition it makes. Instead, it allows for confusion in suggesting that a man can control his own heart. We've seen how a man can blaspheme against the Spirit's work in Christ, but how can a man blaspheme against the Spirit's work in his own heart? In other words, if the Spirit's work in a man's heart is irresistible then how can it also be said that the man can blaspheme against that same Spirit? This is not possible. Until the Spirit changes a man's heart, however, he needs assistance through intercessory prayer so that in the end he does not reject the divine identity and works of Jesus Christ.[234]

Rejection of the Gospel

The third common view of a "sin leading to death" involves knowingly refusing Jesus as Christ. A substantial reference passage outside of John's epistle expresses the possibility of apostasy as follows:

> [4] For in the case of those who have once been enlightened and have tasted of the heavenly gift and have been made partakers of the Holy Spirit, [5] and have tasted the good word of God and the powers of the age to come, [6] and *then*

---

[233] See Eph. 4:30 in which the opportunity for a Christian to sin is clearly implied while also stating that the hope of salvation is maintained.

[234] See Jeremiah 17:9.

> have fallen away, it is impossible to renew them again to repentance, since they again crucify to themselves the Son of God and put Him to open shame. (Heb. 6:4-6)
>
> [26] For if we go on sinning willfully after receiving the knowledge of the truth, there no longer remains a sacrifice for sins, [27] but a terrifying expectation of judgment and THE FURY OF A FIRE WHICH WILL CONSUME THE ADVERSARIES. (Heb. 10:26-27)

Informed by these passages in Hebrews, it is possible that John is describing the heretical teachers of his day as those who committed the "sin leading to death," by which they have "fallen away." (Heb. 6:6) Having "tasted the good word of God" (Heb. 6:5), the "antichrists" of 1 John 2:18-19 willingly left the congregation of believers. So, John's opponents apparently continued to sin "willfully after receiving the knowledge of the truth" (Heb. 10:26), so that they rejected Christ's "sacrifice for sins." (Heb. 10:26) John has argued against heretical teaching throughout the epistle, so near its end he may be emphasizing how serious it is to fall prey to the erroneous educators.[235]

In order to read 1 John 5:16-17 with the understanding that the deadly sin is the rejection of the gospel, it is necessary to recognize that the one who commits "sin *not* leading to death" is referred to as a "brother." The one who *does* commit a "sin leading to death," however, remains

---

[235] It should be noted that the Hebrews passage does not suggest that a true Christian can lose his salvation. First, the context involves reference to elementary teachings and practices in the church of that day. Through those activities it could be said that an unbeliever had been "enlightened," or "tasted the heavenly gift," or "shared in the Holy Spirit," or "tasted the goodness of the word of God" through his experience within the community of believers, yet without himself actually becoming a believer. Second, the author of Hebrews does not say that anyone actually had "fallen away." The entire argument could be a hypothetical case whereby the effects of rejecting Christ's benefits are in very strong language shown to be "worthless and near to being cursed." (Heb. 6:8) For a detailed analysis of these verses see Donald Guthrie, *Hebrews*, in vol. 15 of *The Tyndale New Testament Commentaries*, ed. Leon Morris (Grand Rapids, MI: Eerdmans, 1983), 145.

unnamed.[236] So, we must first understand whether or not the "brother" is a true Christian because the Bible elsewhere rejects the notion that a true Christian can ever fall away from the faith and thereby perish.[237]

The Brother

As we approach the text of 5:16, we first need to understand if the term "brother" refers to man in general, to those merely professing to be Christian, or to those who actually are true Christians. Each occurrence of that term throughout the epistle is accompanied by an exhortation to an individual regarding his own status, but also there is implication regarding another person. What *one* does on behalf of his *brother* has an effect on each of them, both the *one* and the *brother*. Consider the following uses of the term "brother" from the beginning of 1 John.

First, in 2:9-11 John describes that it is possible for one of his "brethren" (2:7 KJV) to stumble because darkness has caused blindness. John Stott notes that ἀγαπητοί used here is best translated "beloved," rather than "brethren" as some versions have it.[238] Whichever translation we use, it is evident that John is not referring simply to fellow man because the ability for one to stumble presupposes that one is walking. Whether that walk is real or pretense only, it is obvious that an unbeliever cannot "stumble" in the Christian walk. So, we are left with the possibility that the author is speaking of true believers, or at least those who imitate true believers.

The remaining uses of the term "brother" are translated from the accusative use of the word τὸν ἀδελφὸν. Such is the case in 3:10, where John states clearly that a person who does not love his brother is a child of the devil, not a child of God. For our purposes, it doesn't matter whether or not we view the term "brother" here as a believer or as fellow man in

---

236 See Aikin, *1, 2, and 3 John*, 210.

237 See John 10:27-29 for Jesus' claim that He cannot lose any who are given to Him.

238 Stott, *1 John*, 99 and 192. Commenting on 5:16 Stott says *brother* is used "in a broader sense either of a neighbor or of a nominal Christian, a church member who professes to be a brother." In his comments on 2:9-11, however, he suggests the term is used for a "true Christian."

general because the subject is "the one," or more pointedly, the "everyone" in 3:4. Whoever "the one" is shall be considered a child of the devil, regardless of whether the "brother" in the predicate of 3:10 is a Christian or not. Although the term "brother" is used here in a generic way, however, we should keep in mind that John may also be referring to any professing Christian.

So far, then, we see the term used once clearly for those at least *claiming* to be Christians, and another occurrence which could be understood as referring to a professing Christian or to man in general. It is important to notice, though, that at this point in 1 John the author is beginning to declare a distinction between the true Christian and the one who only professes to be a Christian. The evidence, John tells us, is in whether or not a person demonstrates the love which he has received from the Father. A true child knows true love, and therefore desires to express that love to others.

Next, in 3:12 John uses the story of Cain and Abel to describe the contrast between a man of darkness and a man of light. These two men are of the same seed biologically, yet opposite seed spiritually. In this illustration John further implies that the *brothers* to whom he is writing may not each be true believers. A person's earthly situation may give the appearance that he is in God's family, when in truth he is of the devil. Someone may have at some point professed to be a Christian, he may have been baptized, and he may even participate in corporate worship regularly. However, those actions do not confirm that he is a child of God.

In 3:13-17 we see "brother" or "brethren" used generally five more times. In each instance the term is the object of the sentence rather than the subject. For example, verse 15 makes a shockingly plain assertion. In paraphrase, it says that "no one who hates his brother has eternal life abiding in him." This reiterates Jesus' teaching that, as far as the law of righteousness is concerned, hatred is equal to murder.[239] John is emphasizing well the effect of the light in not only the external life of the believer, but more importantly in the desires of the heart. As clear and profound as this statement is, however, the subject again is "everyone" and thereby leaves "brother" unidentified.

---

239 See Matthew 5:21.

Though this adds to the developing theme that love for others separates the true and false Christians, we are still left without a clear understanding of the term in question. To this point John has used "brother" specifically for a believer still only once, yet numerous other times in an unspecified manner.

In 4:20-21 we understand that a "brother" is certainly a human being who was alive at that time. Brothers were specific individuals with whom John's reader had contact. Hence, the comparison of man "whom he *has* seen" with God "whom he *has not* seen." Notice that the criteria given here for distinguishing a true Christian is absolute. One cannot say that he loves God and at the same time hate a brother. Even without identifying the brother, it is reiterated that there is no place for hatred in the heart of one who has received God's love. But the term "brother" once again does not necessarily refer to either a *true* or a *professing* believer. So in the first four chapters we cannot know certainly what John means by the term.

Based on John's usage of the term in the fifth chapter, scholars suggest that the author is referring to true believers throughout the entire letter.[240] Though this opinion is valid, our purpose here is to discern John's meaning in chapter five by initially seeing his usage of the term up to that point. Obviously, we can't use chapter five to validate its own preceding context. To do so would result in a circular argument that gives no clear understanding of the passage in question.

In summary, prior to the immediate context of our focal passage the term "brother" is used once for a person *claiming* to be a Christian. All other occurrences can be understood generally or specifically, but we have no clear evidence either way.

---

[240] Michael L. Bryant, "Survey of Recent Research on Prayer in the Fourth Gospel, 1 John, and Revelation" (Ph.D. diss., Southeastern Baptist Theological Seminary, 2008), chp 4, pg 38. Bryant sees all these uses of τὸν ἀδελφὸν as referring to true believers.

The Prayer Which Gives Life

"If anyone sees his brother committing a sin... he shall ask and God will for him give life to those..." (5:16) Having considered who may be the "brother" committing sin, we must now investigate the subject, "anyone," as well as the action that is being encouraged, which is intercessory prayer. To do this we must observe the preceding verses:

> [13] These things I have written to you who believe in the name of the Son of God, so that you may know that you have eternal life. [14] This is the confidence which we have before Him, that, if we ask anything according to His will, He hears us. [15] And if we know that He hears us in whatever we ask, we know that we have the requests which we have asked from Him. (1 John 5:13-15)

The "anyone" being addressed in 5:16 refers back to verse 13, in which John introduces a word of assurance regarding eternal life. Fortunately, he makes clear who should have this hope by an elaborate description of his subject. The recipient of the address is simply ὑμῖν (you). Using a dative of apposition, he then describes "you" as τοῖς πιστεύουσιν (the ones believing). By using this present active participle, he is describing not only believers but also that they are in a continuous state of belief. Furthermore, the object of their belief is "the name of the Son of God." (5:13) They didn't just believe and then doubt, but they *are* and will continue to *be* believers in Jesus Christ. Having established that "anyone" refers to any genuine Christian, the term "brother" here also shares that meaning. After all, for two persons to be brothers implies that they are in the same family. Thus, at this point we are finally able to see that the true Christian, who has not rejected Jesus Christ, commits only sins *not* leading to death.

As we have already seen, John is concerned about validating true Christians while warning against the presence of false ones. Many of the false teachers at one time professed Christ, which seemingly gave credibility to their new teaching. They came from among the members of the early church, but strayed into a lifestyle of unbelief. Though they still held religious views about Jesus, they were blinded by unbelief regarding the true gospel.

The genuine Christian is to have confidence that he will live eternally in the light of Christ. Moreover, his confidence will be strengthened by seeing prayers answered when offered according to God's will. (5:13-14) John uses the future tense verb αἰτήσει in verse 16 to say of the believer that "he will ask." Intercessory prayer is, after all, a natural activity for the child of God who bears in his heart the spiritual fruit of love for fellow believers.[241] This type of prayer is the "channel" by which God sustains life which is inevitably eternal.[242] Thus, a community of like-minded believers will pray for one another, and through their prayers God will sustain both their love for one another and their eternal love for God.

The Sin Leading to Death

It should first be understood that this passage does not suggest using prayer to raise the dead. The life to be given in verse 16 reflects upon the "eternal life" of verse 13. Likewise, the "death" resulting from a certain type of sin must be spiritual, not physical, so that it contrasts appropriately with spiritual life.[243]

Regarding the "sin leading to death," it is likely that John has in view the false teaching which prompted the writing of this letter.[244] Implying through silence that one need not pray in such cases, the teaching of heresy would logically be the most threatening counter-assault on his message of

---

[241] See Aikin, *1, 2, and 3 John*, 207. See also Galations 5:22 regarding fruits of the Spirit.

[242] Bruce Durrelle Smilie, "'Sin Unto Death': A Structural and Exegetical Study of 1 John 5:16–17," (Ph.D. diss., Southwestern Baptist Theological Seminary, 1999), 199.

[243] Aikin, *1, 2, 3 John*, 208. See also John MacArthur, *The MacArthur Study Bible,* (Nashville, TN: Thomas Nelson Bibles, 1997), 1974. MacArthur says that "such a sin could be any premeditated and unconfessed sin that causes the Lord to determine to end a believer's life." He continues to suggest that when God will tolerate no more there is no prayer to prevent the inevitable discipline, which is physical death.

[244] See Painter, *1, 2, and 3 John*, 318 who describes the false teachers as refusing "to make the Johannine christological confession."

what is the true gospel. Moreover, "for life to be given to those who deny Jesus Christ, hate their brother, and refuse the witness of God would be a contradiction."[245]

Developing the traditional view that the "sin leading to death" is a rejection of the gospel, we should consider how John ends this letter just a few verses after our focal passage. He cautions his readers to "guard yourselves from idols." (5:21) Since one of John's main purposes throughout the letter has been to establish Jesus' identity, and in the end he offers a reminder to make sure you know who you are worshiping, it is very likely that the text in between also has to do with proper recognition of deity. The deadliest sin would be one that distorts who Christ is, who He was in the past, and who He will always be.[246]

Furthermore, one who is determined to believe in the wrong Jesus is also disobedient to the Father, and does not love others.[247] The Gnostics saw themselves as superior in knowledge, to the extent that they degraded orthodox Christians instead of loving them. The true children of God, on the other hand, recognize that the only real source for knowledge is the real Jesus. It makes sense, then, that "the fatal sin is what the author's opponents are doing," trading the true Christ for a false idol.[248] While the heretics commit the "sin leading to death," those who follow John's teaching only commit sins "not leading to death."

Rejecting the true confession of Jesus Christ will also disallow its necessary result, love for the brethren. According to John, a child of God will grow in love toward others. And in their humility, these genuine

---

[245] Glenn W. Barker, *1 John*, in vol. 12 of *The Expositor's Bible Commentary,* ed. Frank E. Gaebelein (Grand Rapids, MI: Zondervan, 1981), 355. See also Bryant, "Survey of Research on Prayer," chp 4, pg 40 who suggests that John literally forbids praying for someone who commits a "sin leading to death." This view is based upon the use of the demonstrative pronoun ἐκείνης, which has for its antecedent aJmartiva. Thus, withholding intercession is expected in extreme circumstances.

[246] See Rensberger, *The Epistles of John*, 97 who says that "in the Hebrew Bible, the worship of other gods or a deliberate rejection of God is sometimes spoken of as beyond atonement or prayer (for example, Num. 15:27-31; 1 Sam. 2:22-25; Isa. 22:12-14; Jer. 7:16-20; 14:7-12).

[247] See Marshall, *The Epistles of John*, 248.

[248] Rensberger, *The Epistles of John*, 97.

disciples desire to show love toward one another, just as they understand God has shown love to them in Christ Jesus. Therefore, the "sin leading to death" may be visible in part by a failure to demonstrate the love that would be inherited from the Father.[249]

The Condition of Believers

Scripture makes clear that "the believer is not without sin (1:8), but at the same time he is not characterized by an ongoing sinful lifestyle (3:8-9; 5:18)."[250] This concept, which John has asserted prior to our focal passage, is further emphasized as the reasoning behind intercessory prayer. In verse 17 we are reminded that every believer continues to sin. However, verse 18 claims that "no one who is born of God sins." The Christ he worships is the Savior who "takes away the sin of the world."(John 1:29)

John' intent throughout this letter is "to offer the dual encouragement of empowerment not to sin and restoration when we do sin."[251] Thus, the true Christian need not fear that darkness will overcome him. On the contrary, he will "overcome the world" through the power of Jesus Christ evoked by intercessory prayer. (5:4) In this way, the Christian's sin will not lead to eternal death.

Conclusion

It has been established that in verse 16 "anyone" and "brother" both refer to members of the same visible Christian community. The one committing sin, however, may not truly be a child of God because his

---

[249] Painter, *1, 2, and 3 John*, 319. See also Marshall, *The Epistles of John*, 245 who observes that John has been warning believers against sin that differentiates who is and is not God's child. This understanding makes verses 16-17 a main point, not simply an illustration of prayer.

[250] Aikin, *1, 2, and 3 John*, 207.

[251] Rensberger, *The Epistles of John*, 99.

eternal security rests in the type of sin he is guilty of. So long as the sin is the result of human weakness, not conscious and willful rejection of Christ, the brother's life may be sustained unto eternity through the vehicle of intercessory prayer. Though eternal life is God's gracious gift, His children have the privilege of exercising their ever-increasing love for fellow Christians by petitioning God on behalf of one another. This is an edifying exercise for every believer, and indeed for whole congregations, as they seek to truly conform to the image of the Son.

Though intercessory prayer is a necessary activity in the Christian community, it will be ineffective whenever the request is contrary to God's will. From a human perspective, we can surmise from the defiant actions of apostates that God has left them to the destruction of their own sins. If God has not chosen to regenerate a person's heart, it will remain hardened. And if someone openly rejects Jesus as Christ, though that person may seem to be part of the church, John suggests that it is useless for Christians to pray for the false brother.

Finally, John reminds us that all Christians will continue to sin as long as they are influenced by this dark world. Fortunately, though, by accepting the truth of Jesus' divine identity and works our sins will not result in eternal death. Rather, we live through the atonement and sustaining power of the one who was both God and man – Jesus Christ. So the Christian who has sinned, but has not rejected the gospel of Christ, may receive help to overcome sin in his life through God's answering the prayer of others. For this true child of God, his sin is not unforgivable.

Question 5

How Can God Be Sovereign If I Have a Free Choice in Salvation?

The Issue

Since the earliest centuries of the Christian church, men have debated certain issues over and over again. One such issue involves our understanding of God's sovereignty as it relates to the moral choices of men. If God is completely in control of all things, even the choices made by men, then are men simply puppets to be manipulated by God? Yet, if men truly have freedom of choice then how can it be said that God is sovereign over all things? These are the questions which frame our inquisition for this chapter.

Because of the extensive treatment of this paradoxical topic throughout church history, our logical first step will be to review two prominent, opposing positions which have persisted into present day. Next, I will argue that one of those historical views is the most consistent with God's revelation in Scripture. Then we will consider the legitimacy of opposition against my position. In the end it is our goal not to win a debate, but to seek a better understanding of both God and man so that we may recognize God's glory in it all.

The Positions

In Paul's letter to the church at Ephesus, he gives hope to believers that God "works all things after the counsel of [God's] will."[252] This statement at first seems clear enough. However, when finite human minds attempt to consider the depths of God's sovereignty we find our understanding to be lacking. Of the following major positions, there is little debate that whatever choices humans make they are somehow compatible with God's exercising his full control in the universe. Moreover, it is agreed that because God knows past, present, and future, his will does not adjust as future events take place.[253] As one famous preacher put it, "God sees and knows from everlasting to everlasting all that is, that was, and that is to come, through one eternal now."[254] But as we shall see, there are significant differences of opinion as to precisely how God's sovereignty and man's free choice function together.

Position 1 – Calvinism

Overview. One of the most notorious theologians with regard to the free will debate was John Calvin. Although he lived five hundred years ago, many of his theological positions have been foundational to modern denominations such as the Southern Baptist Convention, which is the largest Protestant denomination in the United States.[255] He argued that

---

[252] See Ephesians 1:11. Unless otherwise specified, all Scripture quotations in this chapter are taken from the NASB translation.

[253] Millard J. Erickson, *What Does God Know and When Does He Know It? The Current Controversy Over Divine Foreknowledge* (Grand Rapids, MI: Zondervan, 2003), 222.

[254] Ibid, 106. Erickson quotes from John Wesley's *Sermons on Several Occasions.*

[255] Thomas J. Nettles, *By His Grace and For His Glory: A Historical, Theological, and Practical Study of the Doctrines of Grace in Baptist Life* (Cape Coral, FL: Founders Press, 2006), 9. See also Thom S. Rainer, "The 15 Largest Protestant Denominations in the United States" [on-line], accessed 29 April 2016; available from http://www.christianpost.com/news/the-15-largest-protestant-denominations-in-the-united-states-92731; Internet. For an overview of some theological differences between many denominations, including those which are distinctively Reformed (Calvinistic), see also

God has fixed all circumstances in the lives of every created being.[256] Every decision and subsequent action taken by man is an effect which results from God's causative will.

Salvation. Perhaps the most heated debates involving Calvinism have to do with God's electing certain persons to salvation while allowing others to continue in their path toward condemnation. According to Calvin, Christians were chosen in Christ before the world was created.[257] He argued that salvation is entirely of God, "not just the gift of eternal life but also the required means by which the gift is received."[258] Election is unconditional, in that God chooses who will have faith in Christ and be saved, so Calvin objected "to the idea that God simply foreknows without having initiative in the matter."[259]

Election, or predestination, is a particular application of God's sovereignty that is an important concept as it illustrates with clarity the paradox between man's free will and God's sovereignty. The key to reconciling these two ends of the salvation spectrum is what Calvinists define as total depravity, in which man is naturally so corrupt that he cannot exercise righteous choices without the aid of God's grace.[260]

Position 2 – Arminianism

Overview. Near the end of the sixteenth century Jacob Arminius argued against some key doctrines which had been prominently held until that time. According to Arminius, "a thing does not come to pass because it has been foreknown or foretold; but it is foreknown and foretold because

---

Gordon-Conwell Theological Seminary Placement Department, "Denominational Chart" [on-line], accessed 29 April 2016; available from http://www.gordonconwell.edu/mentored-ministry/documents/DENOMINATIONALCHART2011-2012.pdf.

256 Arthur W. Pink, *The Nature of God* (Chicago, IL: Moody Press, 1999), 18.

257 Ibid, 18.

258 Chad Brand, ed. *Perspectives on Election: 5 Views* (Nashville, TN: Broadman & Holman, 2006), 81.

259 Brand, *Perspectives on Election*, 83. See also Erickson, *What Does God Know*, 102.

260 Dave Hunt and James White, *Debating Calvinism: Five Points, Two Views* (Sisters, OR: Multnomah Publishers, 2004), 347.

it is yet to come to pass."[261] Those who hold this view would insist that man is completely free to make his own choices, and God allows man to do so. They would argue that God has not fixed all circumstances, but that humans are completely free and able to choose from all options set before them.

Salvation. Subscribers of this view insist that God determines the ends, but not the means to salvation. Regarding election specifically, they would say that "the choosing ones *become* the chosen ones."[262] Their choice is foreknown but not predestined, so that the only thing predestined for them is the *option* which they may choose. Following this line of reasoning, the biblical term *predestine* describes the goal of eternal life, but has nothing to do with God giving faith to a person so that the person may be saved. Thus, God does not choose who will become a Christian and bend their will to respond to the gospel with saving faith. Instead, he simply has predetermined what shall be the fate of those who freely choose to believe in Christ.

The Arminian's main departure from Calvinism is that election is seen as conditional. Salvation is based on who will respond to the parameters God set up for one to become a Christian.[263] Just as man was free to sin, so too he is free to recognize Christ as the solution to man's sin.[264] Foreknowledge is simply God's prediction of what will happen in the future, and he predestines those whom he sees in the future will accept Christ.[265] The gospel is God's free invitation to all who willingly respond; it is universal and resistible.[266]

---

[261] Erickson, *What Does God Know*, 104. Erickson quotes from James Arminius' *Private Disputations*.

[262] Brand, *Perspectives on Election*, 81.

[263] Brand, *Perspectives on Election*, 83. See also Hunt, *Debating Calvinism*, 338, in which Dave Hunt states succinctly that "the natural man has a will that he can turn to God if he so desires is clear from Genesis to Revelation."

[264] Ibid, 84.

[265] Ibid, 85. Hunt refers to Rom. 8:29, 1 Pet. 1:1-2. See also Ibid, 86, in which Hunt argues that the "for" in Rom. 8:29 suggests a progression beginning with foreknowledge.

[266] Brand, *Perspectives on Election*, 121.

Support for My Position

Human Moral Choice is Free

Jesus himself called upon sinners to "repent and believe in the gospel."[267] In order for him to give this command, there must have truly been a decision for his hearers to make. And just a few verses later he again gives the option for people to follow him or not. He even warns people to consider the cost of following him before choosing to do so.[268] His call to forsake everything and follow him, coupled with his warning to be sure we know what we're doing if we do follow him, make clear that his hearers have two options. Repentance followed by lordship is one option, and the other option is to reject the gospel invitation all together.

In addition to Jesus' words regarding the option to repent or not, his apostles carried forth the same teaching and evangelistic proclamations. "And they said, 'Believe in the Lord Jesus, and you will be saved."[269] "For 'everyone who calls on the name of the Lord will be saved.'"[270] "But unless you repent, you will all likewise perish."[271] Even beyond these few examples, throughout the New Testament Scriptures there is a clear call for every man to decide whether to give complete allegiance to Christ or to remain "dead in trespasses and sins."[272]

The key to understanding our moral freedom is to realize that our will is naturally enslaved to sin. Because "the wages of sin is death," and we are sinners by the fact that we were born as humans in a fallen race, we are naturally dead men.[273] This natural state came about because the crucial aspect of the Fall was that the creature desired to "be like god."[274]

---

[267] See Mark 1:15.

[268] See Matt. 8:18-22, 16:24-25, and Mark 10:17-27 for some texts in which Jesus cautions people to consider the cost of following him.

[269] See Acts 16:31.

[270] See Romans 10:13 (ESV).

[271] See Luke 13:3.

[272] See Ephesians 2:1. See also Peter Jeffrey, *New Christians Start Here: Basic Truths for New Believers* (Webster, NY: Evangelical Press, 2005), 6.

[273] See Romans 3:23, 6:23.

[274] See Genesis 3:5.

As with any false god, man cannot create life – not for himself or any other creature. Therefore, man's turning against the one and only giver of life had the natural result of turning toward death. God warned Adam and Eve that death would result from such a decision, but they still chose the idolatrous perversion of self-worship along with its consequences.[275]

This process of rebellion is a legacy that has continued throughout all generations of human beings. Although there is a legitimate choice to be made with regard to following Christ, dead men will always choose what dead men prefer – independence from the giver of life, the Lord Jesus. Just as a dog, given the choice between meat and vegetables, will always choose the meat, we sinners will always choose sin over salvation. We choose sin because salvation involves changing allegiance to Jesus as Lord, whereas we prefer to be lords of our own lives. Unfortunately, we are lords of death whereas Jesus is the only Lord of resurrection.

The question to be answered, then, is how a dead man can desire to live and thereby turn his worship toward the true source of life. "A soul dead in sin must first be made spiritually alive and this is something only God the Holy Spirit can do."[276] This is why Jesus said that "unless one is born again he cannot see the kingdom of God."[277] To be born again is a work of God that man cannot do for himself. Thus, Ephesians 2:1-5 says explicitly that "you were dead in your trespasses and sins… but God, being rich in mercy, because of his great love with which he loved us, even when we were dead in our transgressions, made us alive together with Christ (by grace you have been saved)." Clearly, God takes the initiative to enable a man to make the right choice. Therefore, human moral choice is free but due to our sin nature humans will only make the right moral choice when God graciously enables.

---

[275] See Genesis 3:3.

[276] Jeffrey, *New Christians Start Here*, 6.

[277] See John 3:3. See also J. I. Packer, *Concise Theology: A Guide to Historic Christian Beliefs* (Carol Stream, IL: Tyndale House, 1993), 157. Packer reminds us that the term *regenerate* has been developed to describe this process of the Holy Spirit giving a new spiritual birth.

God is Sovereign Over Human Moral Freedom

Overview. Scripture gives adequate examples of God working in accordance with his will, and doing so with men still making uninhibited decisions. For example, throughout the story of Joseph in Genesis 37-50 we see the results of men making decisions. Joseph's jealous brothers threw him into a well and then sold him into slavery. As the story continues, he was accused of attacking his master's wife and was subsequently put into prison. God then gave Joseph the interpretation of Pharoah's dreams so that Joseph was not only freed but he was also established in a prominent governmental position. With this new authority, Joseph brought his family to Egypt and thus saved them from dying of starvation. In the closing chapters we are not told that the moral of the story is that we should make good choices like Joseph did. Nor is the main point that Joseph had faith throughout trials until God finally decided to use him for something great. Rather, we are told that all along God was exercising his sovereignty through Joseph's decisions, and through the decisions of others, in order to orchestrate deliverance of God's covenant people. Here we have unconditional election in that God demonstrated a particular covenantal love for the people of his choosing. However, we also see many human decisions and their consequences. Even the brothers' evil intentions are accounted as being part of Sovereign God's plan of redemption for his people. In Genesis 50:20, Joseph points out this balanced perspective in responding to his brothers' request for pardon. He says, "*you* meant evil against me, but *God* meant it for good in order to bring about this present result, to preserve many people alive."

Salvation. Calvinists say we must be *born again* in order to have saving faith because we are by nature dead in trespasses, and we are blinded by Satan so that we do not see our need of a Savior.[278] Furthermore, of our own natural ability we can do nothing to please God.[279] This means that regeneration of the heart occurs prior to a person's repentance and conversion.[280] Passages such as John 3:5-8 affirm the idea of a supernatural rebirth, as Jesus himself proclaimed God's initiative in converting otherwise

---

[278] See Eph. 2:1 and 2 Cor. 2:4.

[279] See Romans 8:6-8.

[280] Brand, *Perspectives on Election*, 19.

helpless sinners. Particularly, in verse eight our Lord sympathizes with our confusion in this matter and so offers a metaphor which compares our finite comprehension of God with our ability to see wind. "You do not know where it comes from and where it is going; so is everyone who is born of the Spirit." Moreover, we cannot see wind but we can see the result of its power in the swaying of the tress. Likewise, the effect of the Spirit is evident even though we cannot see the Spirit itself, nor ascertain its origin or destination. We cannot predict when, or under what circumstances, any person will be born again. It is completely out of our control. From a Calvinistic perspective, then, the Spirit regenerates a man so that he will respond to the gospel with repentant faith. This work is in no way initiated by man, but is the gracious action of God alone.

Arminians, however, believe that a man's heart is regenerated as a result of his conversion, which was accomplished as a completely free choice.[281] Notice the difference in the order of events. With Calvinism regeneration occurs first, whereas in the Arminian view man chooses first. Although the word regeneration is a noun, it describes the state of being after an action has taken place. In this case something has been restored, renewed, or regenerated. Thus, the state of regeneration requires that someone has taken action – either God or man.

Those of the Arminian viewpoint struggle with passages such as John 6:44, in which Jesus clearly says that "no one can come to me unless the father who sent me draws him." They would dissect this passage as did Hershal Hobbs, who argued that "draw" is God's initiative and "come" is man's response.[282] His argument, however, remains inadequate to justify a *free will* theology because the question of who God draws is not answered. If anything, he further proves the Calvinist viewpoint by having to stipulate that God's "drawing" *is* God's initiative. This initiative of God's "drawing" is the key point in which Arminians must contend with the Calvinist view.

Furthermore, even Arminians will insist that at the point of conversion a person is moved *by the Spirit*. Under conviction by the Holy Spirit, they would say, a man then chooses to respond. First, can a person have that

[281] Ibid, 19.

[282] Nettles, *By His Grace*, 236.

conviction without the aid of the Spirit? When pressed, Arminians will agree that the work of the Spirit is required, but that some prevenient grace has been given to all humans so that they are just free from sin enough to be able to make a truly free choice in either direction. This assumption of a little bit of grace given to everyone is completely unsubstantiated in Scripture. Moreover, the necessity of any amount of grace further proves that grace must precede one's free choice in salvation. Again, we've come full circle right back to the Calvinistic position that God must take the initiative before a man can choose Christ.

Reaching to justify their position, at this point Arminians are often tempted to then ask if *everyone* has this conviction by the spirit, or if only *some* are drawn. They may also further ask to what extent does the spirit strive, and does he give the same level of conviction to everyone. These questions, however, do not address the issue at hand. Instead, they are simply meant to illicit an emotional appeal based on our worldly perspective of fairness with regard to who is predestined to salvation by God. Moreover, these questions sidetrack us from the root cause of conversion. Regardless of precisely how, when, and within whom the Spirit works, Arminians must agree with Calvinists that the Spirit is necessary or else man is hopelessly lost with no ability to repent.

As much as we want to strictly define the working of the Holy Spirit, our knowledge is limited in the same way that we cannot actually see wind. Just as we believe the wind exists because we see its effects, so too must we acknowledge the work of the Spirit without fully comprehending where he goes and to what extent he will do his work. The point we must keep in mind is that both Calvinists and Arminians agree that the Holy Spirit must move a dead man to repentance and faith. Once this agreement is firmly established, both sides must agree that God takes initiative which then enables man's free choice to be the righteous one.

Objection and Defense

God is Most Glorified in Man's Independence

In objection to my view, it may be argued from the Arminian perspective that God receives no glory from human robots which exert no choice of their own. Only a weak god would have to force his creatures to worship him. Logically, the only way for God to be truly loved and thereby glorified by man is for humans to be given complete freedom to choose God or not. This is the only way for humans to have a personal love relationship with God.

This freedom is evident in the fact that Christians continue to sin after their conversion. If God were responsible for their conversion, and they continue to sin, then God would be proven incompetent to fully do the work he set out to do. Rather, with full responsibility given to humans there can never be a reason to doubt God's power and goodness.[283] Any faults in the lives of believers are because they are human and completely free to make their own choices.

Furthermore, throughout both the Old and New Testaments God repeatedly calls upon people to repent and turn to him. Why would God ask man to *choose* if man does not have any choice to make? In offering salvation to humans, God is implicitly setting up boundaries by which our choice is his preferred way to be glorified. Moreover, it is beside the point for Calvinists to argue for total depravity by using historical figures such as Nero and Hitler as evidence. The Bible is our primary source of revelation from God, and in it he clearly begs for men to turn from sin if they so desire.[284] Man is not a simple puppet, but rather a complex being with complete liberty to choose who he will worship.[285]

The only truly free will must involve the power to choose among various alternatives. If man does not have the ability to make a righteous decision, because he is totally depraved, then in reality he has no freedom

[283] Hunt, *Debating Calvinism*, 335.

[284] See Josh. 24:15, Lev. 19:5, 1 Peter 5:2, and 1 Cor. 7:37 for examples of man's invitation to repent. See also Hunt, *Debating Calvinism*, 336.

[285] Ibid, 339.

at all.[286] Rather, he is enslaved to a taskmaster that does not elicit a loving relationship. God cannot be most glorified if he is not freely loved by man.

God is Most Glorified in Man's Dependence

In defense of my position, Calvinists do argue that man's will is in bondage. However, that will is not in bondage to God via election but instead man's will is in bondage to sin and God's electing grace is what frees us from it.[287] This is why Jesus said in John 8:34-36 that we are naturally slaves to sin but that he can make us free.

The notion of moral freedom is taken to a broad audience in John 3:16-21, in which Jesus says that "whoever believes in him should not perish." He clearly has all of humanity in view by further asserting that "the world may be saved through him." And, the choice that the world has is exercised by individual decisions in that "[a person] who believes in Him is not judged; [a person] who does not believe has been judged already." Clearly, this entire passage reiterates that every person is accountable to respond to the gospel by believing in Jesus. Thus, this is a favorite passage used by Arminians in support of their view regarding free will. In accordance with hermeneutical principles, however, we must also read on to the last phrase so that we do not neglect to receive the author's complete message. Jesus ends this discourse by saying that "men loved the darkness rather than light" but that some will come to the light because their deeds have been "wrought in God." Even here within the most famous passage regarding man's moral choice in responding to the gospel, Jesus clearly states that man's response is rooted God's initiative.

Although Jesus insisted that men have a choice to make, he also says clearly that our will is in bondage. How do we reconcile these two seemingly opposing assertions? We do so by distinguishing *option* from *ability*. The Bible indicates that the *options* from which to choose are certainly and freely available, but humans do not have the *ability* to make righteous choices without aid from the Holy Spirit. So, it is the choices

[286] Brand, *Perspectives on Election*, 100.

[287] Hunt, *Debating Calvinism*, 347.

that are free rather than man's will which is naturally enslaved to choose wrongly.

Human moral decisions are compatible with God's sovereignty because he *calls* us unto himself. He enables us to make right choices of all available options, and by so doing he accomplishes his will without restricting our freedom. In fact, his electing grace gives us true freedom to make choices that we otherwise would not make due to our bondage to sin. As man recognizes his dependence upon God, worship is rightly directed toward him as the source of all righteousness and as the one who deserves all glory. As Paul remarked, "God *calls* us into his own kingdom and glory."[288] Hence, God is most glorified in man's dependence.

Conclusion

Having considered two of the most prominent views regarding God's sovereignty and man's free will in salvation, it has been argued that the Calvinistic position is most consistent with the biblical witness. This does not suggest, however, that opponents to this view are less committed to their Lord, or that they are less useful in the furtherance of his kingdom. As we have done for centuries, may healthy debate on this issue push us to a deeper study of Scripture, a greater knowledge of Jesus Christ, and a passionate desire to see him glorified above all else.

Consider, for example, two outstanding preachers from the Great Awakening of the 1700's. Regarding the topic of predestination, George Whitefield provided for us an example of submitting to John Wesley for the sake of Christ. At a crucial point in the Methodist movement in approximately 1744, both men held firm to their convictions regarding a couple of main issues. One issue was Arminianism versus Calvinism, including the doctrine of perseverance. And the other highly contested issue was the Wesleyan concept of Christian perfection, the belief that a person can be fully sanctified and even become sinless during his earthly

[288] See 1 Thess. 2:12.

lifetime.[289] Whitefield not only had great compassion and respect for Wesley, but he also recognized Wesley's exceptional leadership skills and desire to press forward with Methodism. Although Whitefield had been the preacher to first see great success in the movement, he humbly withdrew from leadership so that Wesley could proceed without division in the emerging Methodist denomination.[290] The two men remained friends for life, and Wesley even preached at Whitefield's funeral.[291]

This historic example demonstrates that the doctrine of election should not prevent us from loving fellow Christians or supporting their work in taking the gospel to the ends of the earth. Instead, let us rejoice that God uses *means* to accomplish his will. Just as he is sovereign over our ability to choose Christ for salvation, so too is he able to ensure the success of the gospel through the meager works and diverse viewpoints of humble men.

---

[289] Arnold A. Dallimore, *George Whitefield: God's Anointed Servant in the Great Revival of the Eighteenth Century* (Wheaton, IL: Crossway, 1990), 64.
[290] Dallimore, *Whitefield*, 153.
[291] Ibid, 197.

Bonus Question

What Can I Do On Sundays?

Introduction

This chapter is considered bonus material because it does not definitively answer the question set forth, and because its source material is limited primarily to the textbooks used for a class on ethics. This "bonus" material is included, however, because it contains introductory ethical concepts which are intended to provoke deeper though regarding the subject at hand. If approached properly, the content herein should stimulate more comprehensive thinking than is typically achieved in traditional Bible study classrooms, thus raising additional questions to be answered by the readers own research.

It can be very difficult for today's Christian to discern which activities are appropriate for Sundays. Some insist that God simply commanded a rest from weekly labors. Others agree to the no-work ethic, but also forbid any secular activities such as sports or other pastimes. Still others say that it doesn't matter what we do on Sunday because Jesus' inauguration of the New Covenant did away with the laws of the Old Covenant.

To add even further confusion, there are just as many views regarding the effect that our observance may have on others. For example, a Christian who wants to avoid working on Sunday may wonder if his dining at a restaurant causes someone else to have to do the very thing he is avoiding. Or, if one refuses to play sports on Sundays he may feel a bit hypocritical when watching games on television. And in another scenario the one who believes he is freed completely from any special observance may question whether or not his life is really any different than an unbelieving neighbor.

It is often presumed that our level of commitment to honoring the Sabbath is a direct reflection of our understanding of Scripture. Moreover, it seems logical that the more devout followers of Christ would be those willing to forego pleasurable activities as proof of their devotion. But these presumptions fall short of what Jesus actually taught about Sabbath-keeping, and likewise they do not reflect an accurate perspective of the Bible's overarching themes.

In seeking what the Bible actually says about Sabbath observance, and how it applies to Christians, it is helpful to approach the subject with a sufficiently broad ethical framework. This investigation is somewhat unique in that it considers biblical arguments from various ethical perspectives. Additionally, the common dilemma of whether or not a Christian should dine at a restaurant on Sundays will be used to illustrate each ethical perspective so that the final analysis will propose a reasonable solution. In so doing, it will be suggested that Christians should freely observe Sunday as the Lord's Day, commemorating their Savior's resurrection, by engaging in acts which foster a fuller appreciation of the eternal rest he affords them, and particularly by being involved in activities dedicated to his worship and the furtherance of his kingdom.

The Fourth Commandment

Moral Law

In keeping with its theme of redemption, the Bible makes abundantly clear that no human, other than Jesus, has ever lived in complete obedience to God. We are quite familiar with the story of Adam and Eve, in which they were the first to sin. Their sin was rooted in a desire to be equal with

God. They ate of the forbidden fruit in order that their eyes would be opened, thus giving in to Satan's temptation that they could be "like God." (Gen. 3:5)[292] This first sin violated the first of the Ten Commandments, which was given hundreds of years later to the Hebrews at Mt. Sinai. (Ex. 20:3) The Genesis story continues with the first children, Cain and Abel. Again we see the breaking of law, the sixth commandment, when Cain murdered his brother. (Gen. 4:8, Ex. 20:13) As human history continued, so did man's acts of unrighteousness, all of which are broadly defined as sin. (1 John 5:17) This characterization of man as having fallen into a depraved condition will be foundational in our consideration of biblical ethics.

When attempting to discern what is morally right and wrong, we often assume that the Moral Law was not given until BC 1446, immediately after the Hebrews' exodus from Egypt. As we've already considered, however, the morality toward which the Ten Commandments pointed was established from the beginning of creation. In fact, God said of the patriarch Abraham that he "obeyed Me and kept my charge, My commandments, My statutes and My laws." (Gen. 26:5) Since Abraham lived over 700 years before Moses, it is obvious that Moral Law did not begin with the Ten Commandments. The commandments are significant, though, in that they were the first written summary of specific applications of Moral Law, but the law itself already existed.[293]

Sabbath in the Old Testament

In the Decalogue, another name for the Ten Commandments, God gave the Israelites specific ways in which they could obey the already existing Moral Law. One of these was the fourth commandment, which states:

---

[292] Unless otherwise specified, all Scripture quotations in this chapter are taken from the NASB translation.

[293] H. M. Riggle, *The Sabbath and the Lord's Day* (Winchester, IN: Gospel Trumpet Co., 1928), 65.

> [8] "Remember the Sabbath day, to keep it holy. [9] "Six days you shall labor and do all your work, [10] but the seventh day is a Sabbath of the LORD your God; *in it* you shall not do any work, you or your son or your daughter, your male or your female servant or your cattle or your sojourner who stays with you. [11] "For in six days the LORD made the heavens and the earth, the sea and all that is in them, and rested on the seventh day; therefore the LORD blessed the Sabbath day and made it holy. (Ex 20:8-11)

As ceremonial laws were developed, restrictions for Sabbath-keeping became as important to the Jewish nation as circumcision. "These two rites were the distinctive badges of Judaism, the marks of distinction from the Gentile world."[294] Moreover, Sabbath was seen as "a sign of special favor of God... the unique distinction of a chosen nation." Although there were drastic penalties for breaking Sabbath laws, keeping the Sabbath served as a guarantee to the Jews of God's mercy upon them as his chosen people.[295] Rather than being burdensome to the Jew, Sabbath laws were liberating because they ensured uninterrupted delight in God and his relationship with creation.

The repetition of the fourth commandment in Deuteronomy 5 indicates that the Sabbath is commemorative of God's gracious deliverance from Egypt.[296] Thus, rather than simply a day of doing nothing, Sabbath was the opportunity to rest in deliverance from bondage. With this in mind, we can see vivid typology joining events and practices of the Old Covenant with fulfillment in the New Covenant. One significant example of this typology is the exodus of the Hebrews from Egypt. That event foreshadowed the coming of Jesus, the ultimate Passover Lamb who would atone for all of mankind's sin and thereby grant freedom from its bondage. Sabbath observance taught God's people to rest in his deliverance, which was to be fulfilled finally and completely in Christ.

---

[294] Paul Cotton, *From Sabbath to Sunday* (Bethlehem, PA: Times Publishing, 1933), 11.

[295] Cotton, *Sabbath to Sunday*, 12.

[296] Gleason Archer, Jr. *A Survey of Old Testament Introduction* (Chicago, IL: Moody Press, 1994), 253.

Sabbath in the New Testament

As important as Sabbath-keeping was in the Old Testament, Jesus taught that strict law-keeping had no saving merit.[297] During most of his earthly life he did observe the Sabbath because he was a Jew, and because he would not fully satisfy the Law's demands until his death. (Gal. 4:4; Col. 2:14) Upon his resurrection, though, Jesus initiated a new age in which the strict observance of Mosaic Law, beginning with the Ten Commandments, would put undue constraints upon a people that had been freed from "the yoke of bondage." (Gal. 4:21, 30)[298] Thus, the Sabbath laws were "no longer binding since the substance (Christ) has come."[299]

"The Sabbath was made for man, and not man for the Sabbath." (Mark 2:27) Not only did Jesus berate the Pharisees for their criticism of his healing on the Sabbath, but he even claimed authority over the Sabbath and every other day of the week. (Mark 2:27-28)[300] In the same account, Jesus demonstrated and taught that helping others did not violate the Jewish Sabbath. In fact, the main concept of Sabbath-keeping has always been to embrace relief from bondage – slavery to man for the Israelites, and slavery to sin for Christians.

---

[297] Cotton, *Sabbath to Sunday*, 147. Cotton points out that though Christianity "rose in protest to legalism," it "became a legalized system" as the movement gained momentum through the centuries.

[298] Riggle, *Sabbath*, 88.

[299] John MacArthur, "Are the Sabbath Laws Binding On Christians Today?" [on-line], accessed 07 Nov. 2008; available from http://www.gty.org/Resources/Issues&Answers/598; Internet. MacArthur also quotes John Calvin as saying that the "superstitious observance of days must remain far from Christians." See also Col.2:17.

[300] Millard J. Erickson, *Christian Theology,* 2nd ed. (Grand Rapids, MI: Baker Books, 2003), 702.

Erickson points out that Jesus' claim to be "Lord even of the Sabbath" emphasizes his deity. Recognizing his deity gives absolute authority to his teaching and actions.

The Lord's Day

There is no command in the New Testament to continue Sabbath-keeping precisely as the Jews had done for generations. However, Christians recognize great significance in what lay behind the original Sabbath observance. A reasonable solution, then, is to observe the pattern of practice in the early church. While the apostles were still alive, they led the new congregations in certain activities on what they called the *Lord's Day.*

They used the term Lord's Day to signify that Christ was ruler of all, as evidenced by the resurrection. Moreover, they dedicated the first day of the week to worshiping their Savior because that was the day on which he arose. Throughout the New Testament the term Sabbath is always used to describe the Jewish tradition on Saturday, whereas the term Lord's Day is consistently used to describe this new weekly observance on Sunday.[301] On this holy day, Christians heard the Scriptures proclaimed, broke bread together, and collected money for evangelistic efforts.

Advocates of strict Sabbath observance on the Lord's Day insist that there is some direct connection between the two. However, their supporting evidence comes from Puritan practices, confessions of faith, teachings of the Church Fathers after the apostolic age, and notions derived only indirectly from their own interpretations of Scripture.[302] Approached without bias, the Bible clearly asserts that Jesus' fulfillment of the Mosaic Law included the inauguration of eternal Sabbath rest. "The covenant he mediates is better." (Heb. 8:6) "There remains a Sabbath rest for the people of God," and "we who have believed enter that rest" by our continued confession of Jesus Christ as our High Priest and mediator of the New Covenant. (Heb. 4:9, 4:3, 4:14) Thus, the Lord's Day of the Christian is

---

[301] Riggle, *Sabbath*, 114.

[302] Iain D. Campbell, *On the First Day of the Week: God, the Christian and the Sabbath* (Leominster, UK: Day One, 2005), 144. Campbell likens the concept of Christian Sabbath to the Trinity, which also is not literally mentioned in the Bible but is a proper concept contained within it. See also Samuel E. Waldron, "Sabbath Series" Sermons and Lectures [on-line], accessed 13 November 2008; available from http://www.samwaldron.us/ sermons_lectures/RBSTETHC-Section3.htm; Internet. Waldron gives significant weight to the teachings of church leaders after the apostolic era.

not carried over from the Sabbath of the Mosaic Law. The term *Christian Sabbath* could therefore be considered illegitimate.

Paradoxically, the New Testament Christian is not bound to the Jewish holiness code for Sabbath observance, yet the Christian's salvation in Christ warrants a much higher level of devotion. This is why the early church joyfully carried out duties of worship and kingdom service on each Lord's Day, giving tribute that their Savior owned every day of their lives. Contemplating the depth of Jesus' work in fulfilling the Sabbath laws should actually result in a more devout observance of the Lord's Day. The Christian has been the recipient of unmatched and unmerited grace, such that he can never sufficiently honor his Savior by worldly deeds on any day of the week.[303]

Ethical Perspectives

It has been established that New Testament Christians have much more reason to set aside a special day for devotion and service to their Lord. The challenge, then, is in discerning what particular actions are permissible. To enhance our discernment, there are several common ethical perspectives which stem from a variety of modern worldviews. Following is a brief exploration of these perspectives, and a consideration of how a person with each perspective may think about our *dining* example.

Ethics of Duty

Deontological Theory.[304] According to this view, moral reasoning is based upon direct commands by God, given in the Bible. Hence, it is also

---

[303] This is not to say that Christians cannot honor Christ by deeds of obedience. Rather, the emphasis here is on the fact that none of man's deeds can bring Christ the full honor and glory that he deserves. The grace we have received is in no way the result of our meritorious acts, so we should be in awe of the Sabbath rest that Christ has earned for us.

[304] James W. Sire, *The Universe Next Door: A Basic Worldview Catalog* (Downers Grove, IL: IVP Academic, 2009), 42. This perspective would come from a person

referred to as the Divine Command Theory. Its objective is to discern right from wrong in modern day, using a standard of right and wrong examples from the past.[305] Proponents of this theory must rely heavily upon the Mosaic Law in order to substantiate ethical judgments. When considering which activities are acceptable on the Lord's Day, there must be a direct connection with the Jewish Sabbath in order to provide clear guidelines. Deontologists, then, must contrive modern-day criteria based upon ancient practices which the Christian is no longer bound to observe.

In this line of reasoning, there is no consideration for how one's actions affect someone else. A man's family being served at a restaurant on Sunday, for example, is to be commended because he is not requiring his wife to cook, nor will his children have any dishes to clean afterward. He is not concerned about the restaurant staff because he is only responsible to obey the fourth commandment in the Decalogue. It is the waitress' own sin that she works on Sunday, and the man is not responsible for her. He is doing what is morally right.

Teleological Theory.[306] This view focuses on the goal toward which an action contributes. Often referred to as the theory of Natural Law, it is believed that every human has a purpose. Moreover, mankind as a whole shares common purposes. Three assumptions are critical: that people have a purpose, that their purpose is evident in the world, and that the purpose or goal of mankind provides the criteria for moral decision-making.[307]

In teleological thinking, harmony within community may be seen as the main purpose of mankind. So, the man taking his family out to eat would be praised for building relationships with his wife and children.

---

holding a theistic worldview. He recognizes that there is a God who interacts with his creation, and who provided direct revelation in the form of Holy Scripture. Accordingly, God expects his creatures to uphold his revealed moral standards, so that our decision-making is grounded in obedience to those standards.

305 Michael Hill, *The How and Why of Love: An Introduction to Evangelical Ethics* (Kingsford, Australia: Matthias Media, 2002), 25 and 46.

306 Sire, *Universe,* 45. This perspective would also stem from a theistic worldview which holds that God has given meaning and purpose to the lives of humans.

307 Hill, *How and Why*, 27.

Furthermore, he is promoting a sense of community harmony by socializing with the restaurant staff.

Consequentialist Theory.[308] A consequentialist praises those actions which satisfy human needs and desires.[309] Thus, right decisions are those that are the most useful to individuals or society as a whole. Because of its emphasis on usefulness, adherents to this theory are often referred to as *utilitarian*. Another term, often applied to them by their opponents, is *hedonist*, from a Greek word for pleasure. Whichever term is used to describe them, consequentialists hold the most individualistic ethical perspective. The entire premise for their thinking is self-focused. A person exists for his own pleasure, and groups of people are to seek the greatest pleasure for the greatest number of individuals within.[310]

This view often falls prey to *liberation theology*, in which the Bible is seen as primarily a narrative of freedom from oppression. It is believed that society's task should be to help disadvantaged people realize happiness in the same way as those more fortunate.[311] Observing a day of rest is physically, mentally, emotionally, and spiritually beneficial to every person in society. Therefore, whether God commands it or not there is a practical necessity for a day of rest to be utilized. Consequentialists would see no mandate that this day must be Sunday, nor would they abide by universal restrictions as to which activities may be appropriate for the day of their choosing. Each person should do whatever helps him to unwind from the busyness of the work week.

With the autonomy of deciding which day best suites his schedule, a man would not be expected to consider the needs of others. His day of rest may differ from that which his wife and children deem most beneficial to them. Therefore, he is only responsible for himself. The waitress at the

---

[308] Sire, *Universe*, 79. As opposed to theism, the underlying worldview here is naturalism or atheism. Because an atheist insists that there is no God, there can be no moral standards placed upon humans. Accordingly, atheists assume that the highest virtue is the survival of the human race, which then becomes the ultimate basis for ethics.

[309] Hill, *How and Why*, 28.

[310] Ibid, 31.

[311] Ibid, 46.

restaurant has no bearing on the man's choice of what is morally right or wrong because it is *his* day, not the *Lord's* Day.

Ethics of Virtue[312]

As opposed to ethics of duty, another main category of ethical analysis is based on virtue. Its target of consideration is the character or disposition of a person, rather than the action performed.[313] With attention focused on the virtuousness of a person, intentions become more important than the result of actions, the goal of the action, or the compliance of actions to any perceived code of conduct.

A virtue ethicist adopts as normative whatever traits are praised by his community.[314] An unbeliever, then, is simply expected to behave like those around him. He must share the convictions of his society, and act accordingly, in order to know that he is doing right. A Christian, in particular, may apply this logic to the smaller church community in which he has close fellowship. According to this view, the man who observes Sunday as a special day is morally right if he is part of a community of others who recognize its significance. However, if he is not part of the Lord's church then he cannot be criticized for failing to observe the Lord's Day.

Furthermore, in modern society a man's commitment to his career is seen to be his defining trait. What a man *does* identifies what a man *is*.[315]

---

[312] Sire, *Universe*, 84. It should be noted that what we are referring to as ethics of virtue involves blending a naturalistic/atheistic worldview with the theistic worldview. Under the influence of both worldviews, a person may be concerned about Sabbath observance (a theistic notion) while at the same time being concerned about the values of his community (a naturalistic/atheistic notion). A purely theistic viewpoint always recognizes God's desires above the desires of human community. Thus, to a theist all virtue originates with God.

[313] Hill, *How and Why*, 36.

[314] Ibid, 38.

[315] Sire, *Universe*, 121. Whether one's worldview is naturalistic or theistic, existentialism often bears its influence. According to naturalistic existentialism, for humans "existence precedes essence; people make themselves who they are." See also 135, in which Sire states that "theistic existentialists emphasize the personal as of primary value." Thus, even a Christian may seek to find self-worth by performing

In this context, observing Sunday as a special day in a secular environment would be wrong because it takes away from the man's identity – his work. He would not be praised by society for refusing to dine at a restaurant because of religious convictions. When a Christian man is around other Christians he should behave according to their standards, but when outside the church he is bound to society's standards.

As for the waitress in the restaurant, she should be working because society demands it. She has chosen her environment, and should therefore submit to its standards. And the Christian patron is free of concern for how his presence may affect the waitress because she has chosen for herself to be identified with society, not his church.

Biblical Ethics

The Bible is not a rulebook of strict protocol, nor is it an obsolete text describing irrelevant ancient history. Michael Hill gives a better perspective of how we should view the Bible.

> "The Bible is God's message of how he has graciously acted in history to reverse the effects of sin and established a new creation… Moreover it is a living word. It is the message by which God continues to reverse the effects of sin and establish a new creation."[316]

As this statement suggests, making morally right decisions requires God's intervention in order to reverse the morally wrong effects of sin. The Bible describes mankind as having fallen into a naturally depraved state, often referred to as iniquity. This condition can be described as being twisted or perverted, not at all what we were created to be. Suffering from this condition since birth, every decision we make is influenced by our fallen condition so that we are prone to follow our innate desires toward

---

deeds in the name of the Lord with whom he has a personal relationship. In contrast, the purely theistic Christian would enjoy serving the Lord simply because of love for the Lord and his glory, not with the added purpose of trying to find self-worth.

[316] Hill, *How and Why*, 49.

their fulfillment in sinful thoughts and actions. Thankfully, God has the power to overcome our iniquity, thus enabling us to make morally right decisions. This *righting of what is wrong* is part of what the New Testament labels good news, or the gospel. Focusing on the Bible's gospel theme, then, enables us to rightly merge some views from common ethical theories into a unified biblical ethic which will guide us toward an ideal Christian perspective regarding what is permissible on Sundays.[317]

Throughout the Bible, including the New Testament, the standard of God's Moral Law is upheld. Jesus said, "Do not think that I have come to abolish the Law or the Prophets; I have not come to abolish them but to fulfill them." (Matt. 5:17 ESV) Not only is the written Law still valid, but men and women are also expected to obey God's unwritten standard of righteousness because "the work of the Law is written on their hearts." (Rom. 2:15 ESV) The Apostle Paul even goes so far as to say that "it is not the hearers of the Law who are righteous before God, but the doers of the Law who will be justified." (Rom. 2:13) The crucial concept for Christians is that, although we are lawbreakers, Jesus is the one and only law-keeper. Through faith in him we "uphold the law" vicariously through his perfect obedience. (Rom. 3:31) But our consideration of the Law does not end there. Rather, our fulfillment of the Law through Jesus Christ is the beginning of a new life of obedience. Our freedom from sin's bondage, which Christ affords to us by his death on our behalf, enables us to live for God. (Rom. 6:10) In fact, Jesus himself makes clear that his Lordship demands our obedience. (Luke 6:46, Matt. 7:22-23, 28:19-20)

Because we are expected to obey our Lord, the Divine Command Theory of ethical decision-making can be helpful if used appropriately. While we should appreciate the desire to be dutifully obedient, a fully biblical ethic requires more than a *works righteousness* that is rooted in our own actions. The Bible clearly teaches that no one is righteous. (Rom. 3:11) But although we are naturally unable to heed the Moral Law, the gospel results in changing the hearts of men so that obedience becomes man's intention. (1 John 2:3-5) Though sin continues to prevent *perfect* obedience, man is still able to honor God with many of his actions by the power of the indwelling Holy Spirit. (Gal. 5:16-26) This is the gracious gift of God

[317] Ibid, 58.

in the New Covenant – that He himself enables obedience to His Law. The Christian's ethical perspective, then, involves simultaneously both a desire to be obedient and an admission to being naturally unable to obey. In this way, we can appreciate the intention of the Deontological Theory in developing our biblical ethic. In our ongoing example, then, whatever we do on Sundays must be within boundaries established by God's Law as revealed in His written Word, the Bible.

Teleological ethicists may see the Bible as useful in some situations, but they believe God's purposes are primarily evident within the reality of a particular situation.[318] This approach by itself falls short because it presumes that sinful people can properly ascertain what God's will is simply by observing natural environments. On the contrary, sin has disrupted the created order within nature. The result is that God's revelation within the Bible is often misunderstood because of sin's effect on the human mind.[319] Moreover, by trying to read nature we minimize the authority of the Bible so that a truly Christian ethic cannot be ascertained.[320]

The teleological approach can, however, add a useful dimension to our biblical ethic. If the purposes we seek to fulfill are rooted in God's Word, then making moral decisions based on His goals is certainly praiseworthy. When Jesus summarized God's Moral Law in the two categories of loving God and loving others, he revealed God's ultimate purpose for mankind – an eternal Sabbath rest in which peace abounds. While abiding in this rest, humans can do God's will by engaging in a love relationship with God, and then expressing God's love to others. (Matt. 22:36-40) Love is both the cause and the desired effect of human existence. (Gen. 2:18) In other words, God's goal for his creation is redemption *of* and *through* love relationships. Accordingly, teleological ethics guided by Scripture would suggest that our activities on Sunday should promote love toward God and love toward others.

Diverging momentarily from considering biblical compatibility of theories categorized as Ethics of Duty, this is a good place to discuss Ethics of Virtue. This category may also have an appropriate influence on

---

[318] Hill, *How and Why*, 47.

[319] Ibid, 69 and 77.

[320] Ibid, 48.

our development of an ethical framework which is biblically supported. Virtue is applicable because it is present not only in the world, but also distinctly within the church. If a Christian understands that he is part of a holy community, he will take responsibility for living according to the standards of that community. Living in harmony with all of God's creation all of the time is a prominent virtue within the church. As a result, Christian love is fundamental in everyday decision-making. (Gal. 5:22, Col. 3:14) Outwardly expressed love, then, will remain a necessary aspect of our biblical ethic. Particularly, though, this love is not because God commands it (deontological ethics of duty) or because it is his purpose for us (teleological ethics of duty). Rather, based on ethics of virtue we love others because that is expected of us in our community. Hence, this theory also exhorts that in our Sunday activities we should engage in demonstrating love toward others.

Let us now return to the third duty-based ethical theory. Perhaps the most difficult ethical approach to merge into a biblical framework is the Consequentialist Theory. Its basic tenet is self-fulfillment and the pursuit of pleasure for oneself alone, which are absolutely contrary to the gospel. Until a person surrenders his own self-claimed right to worldly happiness, he cannot enjoy a right relationship with his creator and therefore he cannot make morally right choices with outward love as his goal. Though the Fall resulted in a break in the love relationship between God and man, and therefore also between man and man, Jesus made possible the restoration of these relationships by offering himself as the atonement for man's sin. This act was the ultimate act of love, done with disregard to his own well-being for the sake of another.

Through Jesus' work on the cross, man can now reenter the intended love relationship with God. And to be at peace with God is to rest in His love, which we can only partially experience as long as we remain in this fallen world. Though Jesus' reign has begun with his first advent, it will not be fully revealed until his return. Therefore, the Christian's "eternal Sabbath is begun but is not fully present" during this age. (Heb. 4:1-11)[321] Moreover, because Jesus is not yet reigning in the heart of every man there

[321] Piper, "Lord's Day"

is not a universally understood concept of God's peace, or Sabbath rest, being what is most beneficial for every person.

During this overlapping period Christians cannot expect all men to rest in Christ because God has not ordained that all men will know him. Therefore, we cannot seek to force God's love and peace upon society – a concept which has been popularly known as the Social Gospel.[322] Only God has the power to change hearts, and he simply commands us to live as salt & light which he will use as he chooses. (Acts 16:14; Matt. 5:13) As we participate in the furtherance of the gospel, however, more individuals will see their greatest need of being made right before God and seek its fulfillment in Christ.

The way to properly apply consequentialist, or utilitarian, influence in biblical ethics is to consider that the ultimate good for mankind is redemption, which can only be attained by *utilizing* the Savior. Rather than being consumed with worldly desires, we must seek to be instruments in furthering his kingdom on earth. And because all of our actions represent him, in every situation we must consider potential consequences for his sake. We must be careful, however, not to confuse actions for the sake of Christ with those which are only for *our* good. Applied in this way, the Consequential Theory can help Christians to make choices that are morally praiseworthy. As pertaining to the topic at hand, we must ask ourselves if our actions on Sundays are in keeping with what is best for both ourselves and those around us. And our final assessment must consider the greatest need of all humans, which is the gospel of Jesus Christ.

Conclusion

Merging the various theories into one multifaceted biblical ethic provides the Christian with a useful process for making moral decisions. First, the church establishes certain virtues as traditionally commendable, which provides the individual Christian with an initial awareness that certain actions may not be morally permissible. He may then search the Bible for

[322] Hill, *How and Why*, 114.

divine commands that strictly forbid the action under consideration. Next, he considers the Bible's overall message that God's goal for mankind is relational harmony under the lordship of Christ. Finally, out of his love for both God and other people he seeks to act in the manner most beneficial for these recipients of his love.

In deciding whether or not the Sabbath can or should be observed today, a Christian begins by considering the virtues existing in his community of believers. Spanning almost 2000 years, the church has established Sunday to be the most appropriate day for corporate worship, as well as private and family devotions. The Christian should therefore set aside the first day of the week for celebrating his eternal Sabbath rest. Searching the Bible for applicable regulations, the Christian finds instead the foreshadowing of eternal peace between God and creation, along with the availability of that rest here and now in Christ Jesus. For the Christian, this *good news* evokes a sense of desire to discard earthly distractions on the Lord's Day in order to bask in the light of the Son. The Christian wants to limit activities to those that honor Christ, foster enjoyment of Christ, and whenever possible help others to know Christ. With love abounding, both for God and for others, Jesus' devoted disciple is at His disposal on this holy occasion. In every way, this day belongs to the Lord.

This position can be further evaluated by applying it to the restaurant analogy. If done out of proper motivation, *patronizing* a restaurant on Sunday is not *patronizing* to Christ.[323] On the contrary, dining out may provide the Christian and his family a wonderful opportunity to simply enjoy the love they share with each other, which was first patterned for them by Christ. Moreover, while enjoying the benefits of Sabbath rest they may also have the opportunity to share the gospel. If the family demonstrates and speaks of the attractive love of God, perhaps the waitress will also seek "the freedom of the Sabbath, that foretaste of our eternal rest with God."[324]

---

[323] The original title of this paper was *"Patronizing the Lord's Day: Christian Sabbath According to Biblical Ethics."*

[324] Mark Earley, "It's About Time" [on-line], accessed 10 November 2008; available from http://www.breakpoint.org/listingarticle.asp?ID=4117; Internet.

Some would argue that the Christian's witness is compromised when he participates in secular activities, such as dining out, on the Lord's Day.[325] However, the argument can also be reversed. If we are witnessing to a gospel of freedom from bondage, it is hypocritical to legalize the day that has been set aside for celebrating freedom. An *unbelieving* waitress has no comprehension of Sabbath rest, and therefore does not have expectations regarding its observance.[326] Furthermore, if Christians withdraw from society then their witness has been removed. For example, if a man refuses to dine at a restaurant for fear of damaging his witness, the waitress he is concerned about will never know that he's not there. She will certainly, then, have no knowledge of his reason for not being there. It is illogical to suggest that one can testify to others without being in their midst. Therefore, freed from strict Sabbath rules the Christian should intentionally represent Christ wherever he goes and in whatever he does.

By gleaning appropriate aspects from numerous ethical theories, while recognizing the authority of Scripture, we have developed a biblical ethic with which to discern praiseworthy activities for Christians on Sundays. We have determined that Christians should freely observe Sunday as the Lord's Day, commemorating their Savior's resurrection, by engaging in acts which foster a fuller appreciation of the eternal rest he affords them, and particularly by being involved in activities dedicated to his worship and the furtherance of his kingdom.

---

[325] Campbell, *First Day*, 196.

[326] The *believing* waitress, it is assumed, has chosen not to work at her secular job on Sunday in order that she may fully enjoy the Sabbath rest which she does comprehend.

Appendix A

Active Repentance – Putting Thoughts Into Action

Introduction

The Apostle Paul wrote his letter to the believers in Colossae in order to warn them against either real or potential false teaching, and to instruct them that being united with Christ should positively affect their behavior. Colossians was written during the same timeframe as his letter to the Ephesians, which results in some shared concepts that help to clarify difficult texts in either book. In fact, their similarities may indicate that both books were to be distributed abroad for general exhortation in the young churches of the region, rather than addressing specific problems of individual churches.[327] Whether particular or general in nature, Colossians expounds many key doctrinal truths which are helpful for believers of every generation.

The source of Paul's concern was likely due to the mix of Jews and Gentiles in these new churches, which inevitably led to disagreement over

[327] See John B. Polhill, *Paul and His Letters* (Nashville, TN: Broadman & Holman, 1999), 329 who notes that about one-third of Colossians is paralleled in Ephesians.

which practices and customs of their previous religions were still necessary, or even acceptable, within the new Christian movement. Paul asserted, though, that believers were freed from all man-made religious stipulations. In the first two chapters of Colossians, he argued staunchly against the enslavement of sacred religious observances. While standing on freedom wrought by grace, Paul called believers to respond to the gospel in the only way acceptable to Almighty God – repentance. (Acts 17:30)

Thus, in the third chapter of Colossians Paul makes a transition from defending the gospel, with particular emphasis on the exalted Christ, to the way in which repentance is evident in the lives of believers. Of particular focus, in 3:1-11 Paul asserts that those who have been raised with Christ will grow in godly wisdom, continually repenting in both mind and deed.

Raised With Christ

Having established the supremacy of Christ and His gospel in the preceding chapters, in his third chapter Paul now gives attention to the application of Christ's supremacy in the whole life of the believer. Paul's admonition in Philippians 1:21 that "to live is Christ and to die is gain" is clearly echoed in Colossians 3:1-4.[328]

> [1]If then you were raised with Christ, seek those things which are above, where Christ is, sitting at the right hand of God. [2]Think about the things of heaven, not the things of earth. [3]For you have died, and your life is hidden with Christ in God. [4]When the Messiah, who is your life, is revealed, then you also will be revealed with Him in glory.[329]

---

[328] All quotations taken from the 1995 NASB translation unless otherwise noted.

[329] NKJV is used for 3:1 mainly because of its more accurate translation of Greek verb tenses. Also, according to Peter T. O'Brien, *Colossians, Philemon*, in vol. 44 of *Word Biblical Commentary*, ed. Bruce M. Metzger (Nashville, TN: Thomas Nelson, 1982), 161, and Daniel B. Wallace, *Greek Grammar, Beyond the Basics: An Exegetical Syntax of the New Testament* (Grand Rapids, MI: Zondervan, 1996), 647, καθήμενος

To Die is Gain

In Colossians 2:20 Paul explained that believers "died with Christ to the elementary principles of the world," and are therefore not to "submit [themselves] to decrees." This warning against legalistic outward behavior is clearly in view at 3:1. Hence, the subordinating conjunction Εἰ οὖν (therefore) introduces the counterargument that the conduct of those "raised with Christ" should be described as "seeking those things which are above" instead of seeking to obey regulations of earthly religions. Christians have died to everything earthly, including false religion.

Paul understood clearly that the death of flesh is the only means for entering into the new covenant. In the old covenant man's response in faith was to destroy a part of his flesh through circumcision, while the remainder of his deserved death was taken by an innocent substitute – the animal sacrifice. The new covenant, being a much "better covenant" (Heb. 8:6-13), requires the faithful response of man killing his entire body. This complete death is physically impossible for humans to accomplish without neglecting God's purpose for them to live as His image-bearers on the earth. (Gen. 1:27) Therefore, Jesus Christ gave his own life in order to ransom the elect from the bondage of the old covenant, which was aptly described as a "ministry of condemnation." (2 Cor. 3:9-14) By His physical death Christ has become the circumcision of the believer's entire body of flesh. (2:11) What has taken the place of circumcision, then, is the death of the whole man, through one man, Christ Jesus. The circumcision of the

---

(sitting) does not immediately follow ἐστιν (he is), so it is not periphrastic. Hence, the phrase οὗ ὁ Χριστός ἐστιν ἐν δεξιᾷ τοῦ θεοῦ καθήμενος (where Christ is, sitting at the right hand of God) is best translated as two dependent clauses. NLT is used for 3:2 primarily for consistency of heaven vs. earth imagery. Particularly, NET was avoided because its translation of φρονεῖτε as "keep thinking" rather than "think about" utilizes aktionsart theory rather than verbal aspect theory. ESV is used for verse 3:3 because of its better rendering of verb tense for ἀπεθάνετε (you have died), and its inclusion of the comma helps the reader to follow the flow of Paul's argument. HCSB is used for 3:4 because "your life" is the more literal rendering of ἡ ζωὴ ὑμῶν, as opposed to "our life" as some versions have it. Also, the passive voice in φανερωθήσεσθε is better translated "is revealed" than "appears." It would have been better, however, to translate ὁ Χριστὸς as "Christ" instead of "Messiah." All other popular translations render it in this way.

new covenant is our willingness to die figuratively along with Christ, on the basis of *faith* in Christ. Although water baptism has great significance and symbolism in this regard, death alone is what unites us to Christ.[330]

In the death of Christ is the death of death itself.[331] He is not only the sacrificial lamb, our complete circumcision, but He is also the reigning king and conqueror. The acknowledgement that Christ is "sitting at the right hand of God" (3:1) not only expresses the high position of Jesus, but it also echoes the triumphant call of Psalm 110. There "God commands the Davidic ruler to 'sit at his right' until God subdues all of the ruler's enemies and subjects them as a 'footstool' for the ruler's feet."[332] Paul was convinced that Jesus is ruler of all (1:15-20), such that the enemy and all his evil deeds are overcome by Christ.

It is therefore understandable that Paul sees victory over darkness as an integral part of every believer's daily life. Our union with Christ involves putting to death sin in our own lives.[333] Because "he who has died is freed from sin" (Rom. 6:7), every believer must die to his earthly existence in order to be united into Christ's body of heavenly existence. The enemy is thus destroyed one life at a time, being overcome by Christians "putting to death" (3:5) whatever wickedness remains in their lives. In this way, the power of Christ is evident in the lives of believers now, which is only a shadow of His power to be revealed at the end of time.

---

[330] See Christopher A. Beetham, *Echoes of Scripture in the Letter of Paul to the Colossians*, in vol. 96 of *Biblical Interpretation Series*, ed. R. Alan Culpepper and Ellen van Wolde (Boston, MA: Brill, 2008), 225 who argues that water baptism is what unites us to Christ. This view takes "buried with [Christ] in baptism" (2:12) to be literally equivalent to Old Testament circumcision, which negates Paul's assertion in 2:11 that ours is "circumcision not made by hands." Water baptism *is* made by hands. It could be argued, however, that baptism in the Spirit is the new circumcision (2 Cor. 1:22, Matt. 3:11), yet Paul would still insist that the indwelling Spirit results in the death of the "old man." (Eph. 4:22-23 HCSB) Beetham agrees, though, that "the Colossian faithful were circumcised in Christ's circumcision."

[331] This phrase was borrowed, and slightly altered, from John Owen's book titled *The Death of Death in the Death of Christ*.

[332] See Beetham, *Echoes*, 221.

[333] Though the new covenant is of grace, God has designed it so that man participates, and yet is only *enabled* to participate, by the indwelling presence of the Spirit. (Eph. 3:16-17)

To Live is Christ

Continuing the concept of resurrection power in the life of a believer, Paul's exhortation in 3:1 to "seek those things which are above" involves an ongoing process of both thinking and acting with a *repentant* perspective. In short, this new life *through* repentance is a new life *of* repentance. Therefore, he follows in 3:2-11 with a chiastic structure, telling us what we should and should not do in this new life. We are to stop sinning against God and against man, doing so by controlling our thoughts, on the basis of our new life in Christ. Thus, the ABBA structure of the chiasm can be summarized as such: *think* in conformity to heaven (A_1), *act* not in conformity to earth (B_1), *act* not in conformity to the old man (B_2), and *think* in conformity to the new man (A_2).[334]

Though including much additional detail, the basic purpose of 3:2-11 is to explain the means by which the repenting action of 3:1 is to be accomplished. Supporting this argument is Paul's usage of verbal aspect in each section of the passage. In 3:1 he uses the aorist συνηγέρθητε (raised) and present tense ζητεῖτε (seek), both with regard to actions in the believer's life. Then, 3:2-11 in proper chiastic form expounds upon his exhortation with the present φρονεῖτε (think), aorist Νεκρώσατε (put to death), aorist ἀπόθεσθε (put off), and present ἀνακαινούμενον (being renewed). Of further interest, these same verbs progress from active to middle to passive voice in the last section. It is as if Paul is saying imperatively with the first two aorists that believers must be involved in actively thinking specific thoughts (present, imperfective aspect), while generally shunning sins against God (aorist, perfective aspect). This is the first A_1B_1 portion of the chiasm. In the final B_2A_2 segment he uses the aorist imperative again to describe a general shunning of sins against fellow believers, but the middle voice is utilized to emphasize that what has been commanded so far has been the sole responsibility of humans. This prepares the reader for the climactic use of a present participle, again regarding the acquisition of a specific kind of knowledge, but this time uniquely with the passive voice. The surprising point, then, is that thinking in conformity with heaven,

---

334 See Appendix B for a detailed tracing of the entire passage, with notations regarding the chiasm.

which he commands believers to do, is ultimately enabled by God. This passive verb ties right back to the passive συνηγέρθητε (raised) of 3:1.

Just as the believer has been "raised with Christ" by grace, so too is the believer "being renewed in knowledge" so that he may continue to grow in grace. Of first priority, then, is for the believer to have a heavenly perspective which is grounded in new life with Christ.

Think in Conformity to Heaven (A₁)

Paul is concerned that Christian actions are to be driven by heavenly goals, rather than by earthly religious customs. In order for heavenly goals to drive actions, though, 3:2 states that the mind must "think about the things of heaven."[335] In short, thinking affects living.[336] Paul clarifies this dual concept of heaven-seeking in 3:2-4, in which he asserts significant detail with regard to heavenward thinking.

In 3:3 we see the two-fold aspect of the gospel. Jesus could not die without being raised, nor could He be raised without dying. In the same way, those who are reborn with Him unto eternal life must also die first or else they cannot be raised.[337] Believers die to self and live to Christ, a transformation hidden in Christ until revealed in glory. This is the ground for heavenly thinking.[338]

---

[335] See O'Brien, *Word*, 163-164 who states that Paul uses the root of φρονεῖτε 23 times of its 26 New Testament occurrences. Of his various uses the basic idea is to *give one's mind to.*

[336] See Rom. 8:5-6, which also refers to the activity of the Holy Spirit.

[337] James G. Dunn, *The Epistles to the Colossians and to Philemon: A Commentary on the Greek Text* (Grand Rapids, MI: Eerdmans, 1996), 203.

[338] O'Brien, *Word*, 171. See also Dunn, *Epistles*, 208 who argues incorrectly for the notion of vindication being part of this anticipation toward revealed glory. He suggests that believers should find comfort in knowing that some day others will see them for who they really are in Christ. This position is contrary to the fruits of the Spirit, in which vindictiveness has no place. Rather, Paul's comment here regarding revelation in the parousia simply explains the time in which our hiddenness will be revealed, so as to clarify the concept of being hidden in Christ.

Dunn suggests that the repetition of the present tense ζητεῖτε (seek) in 3:1 and φρονεῖτε (think) in 3:2 indicates a "sustained effort of perspective."[339] However, considering the other present active verbs in verses 1-4 Dunn's position is an exaggeration. At the end of 3:1, for example, if Paul's readers understood the present tense ἐστιν (he is) to be durative in aspect he would not have needed to include the participle καθήμενος (sitting).[340] Present tense does not always mean durative, or stative, in aspect. A better argument for the durative aspect is that the chiastic complement to φρονεῖτε is the present passive participle ἀνακαινούμενον (being renewed) in 3:10. Structurally, in the chiasm A_1 must assert the same basic idea as A_2. Therefore, the participle controls the meaning of both phrases.

Paul continues in 3:4 to describe how a believer's past action of conversion results in an ongoing present transformation with the promise of future glorification with Christ. As Dunn notices, there are three tenses used with regard to salvation: raised with Christ (past tense), hidden with Christ (present tense), and revealed with Christ (future tense). The Messiah, then, "is our life" completely.[341] Garland points out that because Christ rules all, as described in 3:1, our lives are included in that rule.[342]

---

339 Dunn, *Epistles*, 205.

340 See Mark A. Seifrid, "Tense and Aspect" (classroom lecture notes, 22440A – *Greek Syntax and Exegesis*, Fall 2008, photocopy), 17 for a description of the durative aspect in the aktionsart theory.

341 See Eduard Lohse, *Colossians and Philemon: A Commentary on the Epistles to the Colossians and to Philemon*, in *Hermeneia: A Critical and Historical Commentary on the Bible*, ed. Helmut Koester (Philadelphia, PA: Fortress Press, 1971), 134 who prefers "our life," presuming that a change was made early in order for the text to conform to the rest of the letter which is in second person. He also seems to base his decision partly on interpretations by church fathers such as Ignatius. See also Bruce M. Metzger, *A Textual Commentary on the Greek New Testament* (Freiburg, Germany: United Bible Societies, 1994), 557 who prefers "your life" due to stronger manuscript evidence, particularly p46, along with significant representation in Alexandrian and Western texts. "Our life" conforms to surrounding usage, which sometimes is evidence for alteration to match. However, in this context using "our" could allude to apostles only whereas he is clearly speaking to all believers. An equally plausible theory is that in copying early MSS the word was either read or heard incorrectly.

342 David E. Garland, *Colossians and Philemon: From Biblical Text… To Contemporary Life*, in *The NIV Application Commentary*, ed. Terry Mack (Grand Rapids, MI: Zondervan, 1998), 202.

If we are to think heavenward, in which Christ is the central authority, it is fitting that the hymn of 1:15-20 be included immediately after Paul's introduction. This section of the letter gives the reader, or hearer, a specific description of the type of godly knowledge that strengthens one's faith toward God and love toward people. By focusing on the supremacy of Christ (1:16, 2:10), and by focusing on Christ as head of the elect (1:18), we are more inclined to love other believers than to sin against them (3:7-10).

Already/Not Yet

After the transitional verses of 3:1-4, the remainder of the letter is a call to proper Christian actions, which can be taken either as soft potentialities or as firmly rooted realities. In other words, a true believer either demonstrates an ongoing process of dying and being raised, or the believer has already completely died and has been raised to a totally new lifestyle. To understand Paul's intended meaning, it is necessary to ascertain his usage in 3:1 of the aorist tense for συνηγέρθητε (you were raised).

Since the late nineteenth century the term *aktionsart* has been used to describe Greek verbal aspect. According to this tradition, the aorist indicates an event that occurred completely in the past with no continuing result.[343] For actions that occurred in the past but did have abiding results, the present tense was thought to convey what has come to be described today as *stative* aspect.[344] In recent years, though, the terminology of perfective versus imperfective verbal aspect has found its place in the realm of exegesis. This view proposes that instead of when in *time* an action took place, or what *type* of action took place, the goal of verbal inflection is to assert the author's perspective, or viewpoint, of the action. The aorist, for example, would be described as *perfective* and characterized by *remoteness* in past, present, or future tenses. Another way to describe the perfective aspect would be that the author saw the action from a bird's eye view,

---

[343] Constantine R. Campbell, *Basics of Verbal Aspect in Biblical Greek* (Grand Rapids, MI: Zondervan, 2008), 27.

[344] Stanley E. Porter, *Idioms of the Greek New Testament* (London: Sheffield Academic, 1999), 21.

or that he saw the big picture of what happened from a distance.[345] The present and imperfect tense-forms, on the other hand, may be described as *imperfective* in aspect, in which the author describes the action as if it were "unfolding before the eyes."[346] The imperfect tense-form is regarded as having the spatial value of *remoteness*, whereas the perfect tense-form has the spatial value of *proximity*.

Throughout his writings, Paul asserts the reality that "if anyone is in Christ he is a new creature" (2 Cor. 5:7). Following the context of Colossians so far, Paul sees believers as being "*filled* with the knowledge of His will" (1:9, emphasis mine), "bearing fruit in *every* good work" (1:10, emphasis mine), "having been buried... also raised" (2:12), "you were dead... [but] He made you alive" (2:13) – all implying that a definite and complete transformation has taken place. Following the aktionsart convention, in 3:1 the aorist συνηγέρθητε should be translated "you were raised," indicating that the believer has indeed been completely transformed from death into new life τῷ Χριστῷ (with Christ) at some point in the past.[347]

The next proposition, however, seems to contradict the aktionsart view of aorist usage. In order for the believer to "seek those things which are above" there must be an abiding result of the transformation that has taken place.[348] Furthermore, other Pauline writings would suggest that being "raised with Christ" is an instantaneous action with both completed and ongoing results. Describing the aorist here as perfective in aspect and remote in state would be fitting, as the entire sentence is a bird's eye view of both past action and present state. This concept of having been raised, while yet being raised, is often referred to as an already/not yet tension – that believers have been fully reborn into the heavenly kingdom, but have not left the earthly realm.

---

345 Campbell, *Basics*, 37-38.

346 Ibid, 40.

347 See O'Brien, *Word*, 159 who points out the article of renewed mention in τῷ Χριστῷ (in Christ). See also Garland, *NIV*, 202 who notes that this usage often means "belonging to the world above."

348 See O'Brien, *Word*, 160 who states that the verb denotes continuous effort. However, NKJV was selected for "seek" because context indicates continuous action rather than using English adjectives to enforce an aktionsart or stative notion that the present tense is always durative.

Act Not in Conformity to Earth (B_1)

Even while in the earthly realm, believers who focus their thoughts upon Christ will conform less and less to the world. Their actions will resemble heavenly citizens rather than earthly men.

Paul utilized a rhetorical method common among stoic philosophers of his day, in which vices and virtues were listed in groups of five. Some examples, to name a few, include his description of the contrast between sinful acts and fruits of the Spirit (Galatians 5:19-23), qualifications for leaders (1 Tim. 3:2-13), and rules of household order (Col. 3:18-4:1).[349]

> [5]Put to death therefore what is earthly in you: sexual immorality, impurity, passion, evil desire, and covetousness, which is idolatry. [6]Because of these, the wrath of God is coming. [7]In these you too once walked, when you were living in them.

This list is comprised of sins primarily against God himself. The believer who is focusing on Christ and is thereby growing in godly wisdom will demonstrate an ongoing repentant attitude by stopping a lifestyle of sinning against God.

Act Not in Conformity to the Old Man (B_2)

This section focuses on a general list of sins believers often commit against one another. Because they are to live in community as one unified body, they must put off any sin that disrupts harmony.

> [8]But now you yourselves are to put off all these: anger, wrath, malice, [slander], filthy language out of your mouth. [9]Do not lie to one another, since you have put off the old man with his practices.

---

[349] Polhill, *Letters*, 14.

Repentance involves stopping a lifestyle of sinning against other Christians. All the members of Christ's body must work together for His glory. To do so requires members who are being "renewed in knowledge" so that they may be "the image of [their] Creator." (3:10)

Think in Conformity to the New Man (A$_2$)

The "knowledge of His will" is necessary in order to live "in a manner worthy of the Lord." (1:9-10) This worthy living is the bearing of fruit (1:10), which had taken place because of the gospel (1:6), and particularly because the believers "understood the grace of God" in the gospel. (1:6) Somehow this knowledge of God is tied to "being strengthened with all power" (1:11) in order to live as prescribed. So, in 3:10 the stative aspect and passive voice of ἀνακαινούμενον (being renewed) indicate that believers are continually growing in godly wisdom by Christ's own initiative and power. He is the giver of wisdom which enables repentance.

There is a two-way relationship between knowing and doing. Just as sins hinder the knowledge of God, so too the knowledge of God hinders sin. Therefore, the more a believer focuses upon Christ and His cross, the more sin can be suppressed. And the more sin is suppressed, the more knowledge can be attained.

> [10]and have put on the new man, who is being renewed in knowledge according to the image of his Creator. [11]Here there is not Greek and Jew, circumcised and uncircumcised, barbarian, Scythian, slave, free; but Christ is all, and in all. (3:11)[350]

Jesus Christ "is the propitiation for our sins; and not for ours only, but also for those of the whole world." (1 John 2:2) Paul makes this assertion

---

[350] ESV is used for 3:10 because ἐνδυσάμενοι is more accurately translated "have put on," even though aorist. "Put on" would seem imperatival. Also, "new man" is the more accurate rendering of τὸν νέον, and corresponds better with the old man/ new man theme.

with very few words in 3:11, stating that "Christ is all." Throughout the Bible one can find many truths for which this phrase could be the summary. Limiting ourselves to the immediate context, though, Paul is summarizing here that Christ is the means by which the "old man" is to be "put off." (3:9) He is the "new man" and "renewed… image" whom we are seeking to imitate (3:9), and is the entire purpose of "our life." (3:4)[351] Beetham states simply that "believers have entered the new creational age as part of the new humanity wherein Christ pervades as prototype, source, and sovereign."[352] Paul was so convinced of the primacy of Christ in the whole life of believers that he elsewhere stated "If we live, we live to the Lord; and if we die, we die to the Lord. Therefore, whether we live or die, we belong to the Lord." (Rom. 14:8 HCSB)

No religious practices, good works, or anything other than the gospel can appease God's wrath. Therefore, the believer recognizes that his purpose in life is consumed with Christ. To the believer, "Christ is all." Furthermore, all earthly distinctions are broken as Christians become one in the body of Christ. We are truly a new creation, with a new focus – Christ. He is our source and our goal. "[He] is all, and is in all." (3:11)

Conclusion

Not only was Paul the apostle "to the Gentiles" (Acts 18:6), but he was also "a Jew." (Acts 22:3) He was therefore qualified, and certainly compelled, to exhort the Colossian Christians to uphold the true gospel of Christ and not be subject to competing traditions. In doing so, he was careful to articulate that a different kind of circumcision had been established for God's children in the new covenant.

Believers who have been raised by the circumcision of Christ's death are "being renewed in knowledge" (3:10) by "[seeking] things of heaven" (3:1) and living in active repentance. Reborn to new life in Christ and continually maturing in the faith, they will put off the old man and put

---

[351] See Lohse discussion of "our/your" in note 341.

[352] Beetham, *Echoes*, 226

on the new man by putting to death sins against both God and man. Faith toward God and love toward others therefore comes from an active hope toward heaven. (1:4-5) In summary, those who have been raised with Christ will grow in godly wisdom, continually repenting in both mind and deed.

Appendix B

Following is a *tracing* of Colossians 3:1-11. The practice of tracing is typically employed by Bible teachers and pastors in order to properly ascertain the meaning of a biblical passage, and to help establish a suitable outline for conveying its message to others. This exercise involves breaking the passage down into individual *propositions*, which are simply the smallest phrases that actually say something. Once identified, the propositions are separated visually and then connected together by identifying how they are related to one another. Key words, which I've underlined in this example, can be helpful in determining the relationship between each proposition. In addition to the presence of normal tracing symbols, this example also identifies the ABBA structure of the chiasm described in Appendix A. For a more detailed explanation of the tracing process, see Thomas Schreiner's book *Interpreting the Pauline Epistles.*

Appendix B

Tracing of Colossians 3:1-11

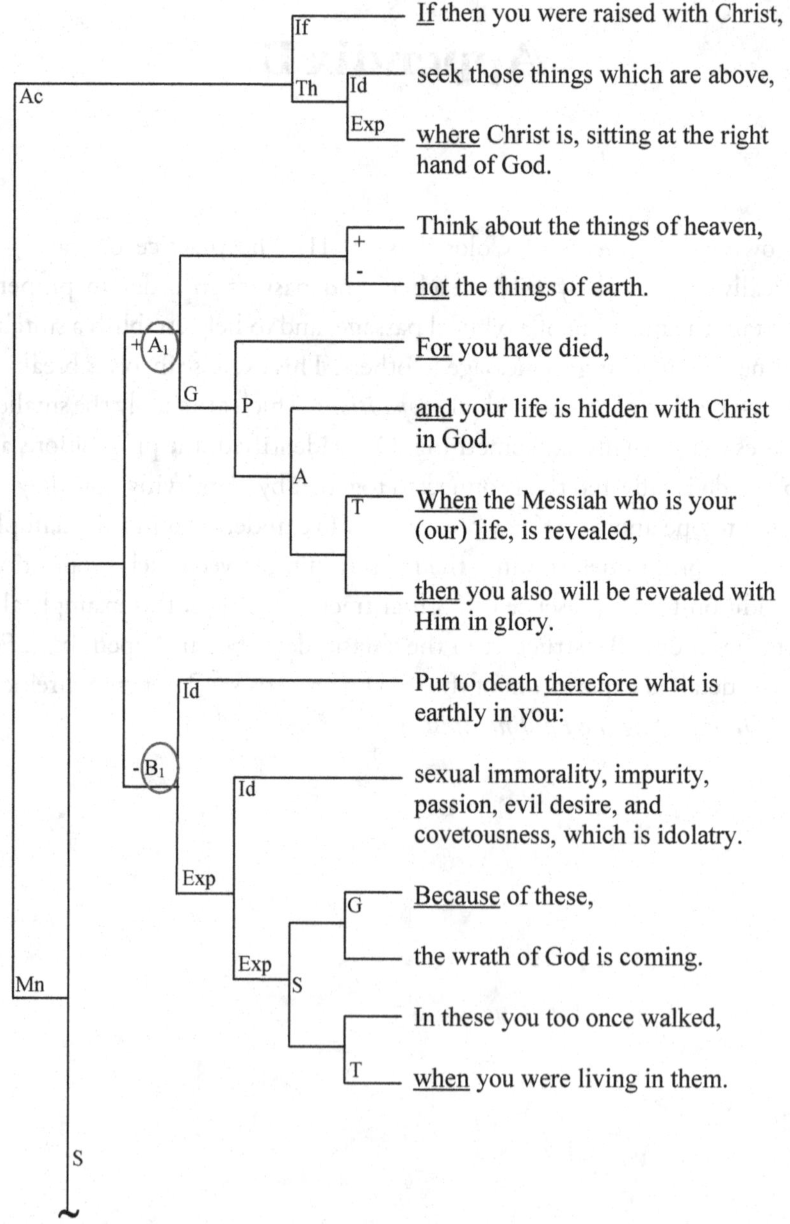

If
Th
Id
Exp
Ac
+
-
+ A1
G
P
A
T
- B1
Id
Exp
Id
Exp
G
S
T
Mn
S
If then you were raised with Christ,
seek those things which are above,
where Christ is, sitting at the right hand of God.
Think about the things of heaven,
not the things of earth.
For you have died,
and your life is hidden with Christ in God.
When the Messiah who is your (our) life, is revealed,
then you also will be revealed with Him in glory.
Put to death therefore what is earthly in you:
sexual immorality, impurity, passion, evil desire, and covetousness, which is idolatry.
Because of these,
the wrath of God is coming.
In these you too once walked,
when you were living in them.

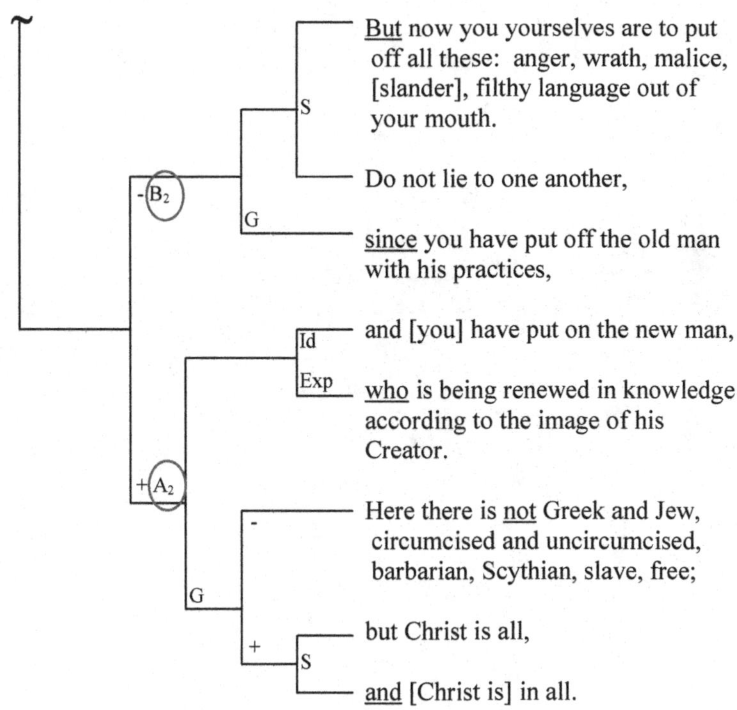

Key:

Id/Exp	Idea/Explanation	A	Alternate
If/Th	If /Then	G	Ground
+/-	Positive/Negative	P	Progressive
Ac/Mn	Action/Manner	S	Series
		T	Temporal

But now you yourselves are to put off all these: anger, [illegible] malice, [slander], filthy language out of your mouth.

Do not lie to one another,

since you have put off the old man with his [deeds],

and [have] put on the new man,

who is being renewed in knowledge according to the image of him who created him,

Here there is not Greek and Jew, circumcised and uncircumcised, barbarian, Scythian, slave, [free],

but [illegible]

and Christ is [in] all.

Printed in the United States
By Bookmasters